INDIAN POETRY

INDIAN POETRY

ROMESH DUTT, C. I. E.

GYAN

Published by

Gyan Publishing House
5, Ansari Road
Daryaganj, New Delhi-110002
Phone: 011-47034999, 9811692060
E-mail: books@gyanbooks.com

Distribution Network
gyanbooks.com
India, USA, Canada, UK, Australia, France

ISBN: 978-81-212-8670-1 (PB)
First Published, 1905

2nd Impression 2023

Printed at: Gyan Press, Delhi.

INDIAN POETRY
Author: Romesh Dutt

Sarasvati — The Indian Goddess of Poetry.
(From a Picture designed by the Calcutta Art Studio. — with permission)

INDIAN POETRY

SELECTIONS RENDERED into ENGLISH VERSE

by ROMESH DUTT · C · I · E ·

· MDCCCCIV · PUBLISHED · BY · J · M · DENT · AND · CO : ALDINE · HOUSE · LONDON · W · C

CONTENTS

I.—HYMNS OF THE RIG VEDA

II.—PASSAGES FROM THE UPANISHADS

III.—PASSAGES FROM BUDDHIST LITERATURE

IV.—THE BRIDAL OF UMA, BY KALIDASA

V.—THE PENANCE OF ARJUN, BY BHARAVI

I

HYMNS OF THE RIG VEDA

Date, circa 1500 B.C.

"The Rig Veda consists of 1028 hymns, comprising over ten thousand verses. The hymns are generally simple, and betray a childlike and simple faith in the Gods, to whom sacrifices are offered and libations of the Soma juice are poured, and who are asked for increase of progeny, cattle, and wealth, and implored to help the Aryans in their still doubtful struggle against the black aborigines of the Punjab."

—*Civilisation in Ancient India.*

HYMNS OF THE RIG VEDA

I

INDRA, THE RAIN-GOD

Vritra is supposed to confine the waters, and will not let them descend until the Rain-God, Indra, strikes the monster with his thunderbolt. The captive waters then descend in copious showers, rivers rise almost instantaneously, and gods and men rejoice over the changed face of nature.

1

Vritra is the rain-withholding cloud. Indra rends the cloud by lightning and pours out rain

I WILL sing the wondrous story,—
Thunder-arméd Indra's glory,—
How he won from Vritra's might
Captive waters sparkling bright,
Cleft for them the mountain way,
Rolled the rivers rich and gay!

2

Indra pierced the dragon cloud,—
Darkening mountains in a shroud,
Twashtri forged the lightning-dart,—
Fashioned with celestial art,
As the milch-kine to the fold
Rivers to the ocean rolled!

Libations of the juice of the Soma plant were given to the gods

3

Like a bull, impetuous, strong,
Indra, hymned in ancient song,
Drank the Soma three times given,
Grasped the forkéd brand of heaven,
Smote the first-born fiend of might,
Rolling up the mountain's height!

4

Indra! When you slew the first-born,
Cleared the shadows of the red morn,
When with bright flame-fashioned arms
You dispelled his spells and charms,
Leaped the light of ruddy dawn,
Foe or fiend of gloom was none!

5

Darkling Vritra hid the world,
Lightning-lances Indra hurled,
And his thunders' deadly stroke
Clouds to pieces rent and broke,
Like a tree by woodsman felled
Fell the fiend by Indra quelled!

6

Feeble foe, by madness fired,
Combat with the strong desired;
Many-slayer, stout of hand,
Indra hurled his restless brand;
How the vanquished splashing fell,
How the streams did roar and swell!

The cloud is represented as a Titan, battling with Indra

7

Footless, handless, in his rage
Vritra still the war would wage;
On his shoulders deep and broad
Fell the thunders of the God;
Boastful but emasculate,
Crushed and torn he sought his fate!

8

Like the leaping wild cascade
Torrents rolled above the dead;
Erst the coiling fiend of gloom
Compassed waters in his womb,
Prostrate now and low he lay,
Rivers laughed in boisterous play!

9

Mother rain-cloud gathered new,
Indra to the combat flew,
Hurled new thunders dark and dun,
Smote the mother like the son;
As the calf beside the cow,
Whelp and dam alike lay low!

10

Rolled the rivers fresh and new,
Ceaseless waters onward flew,
Bursting torrents, copious fed,
Bore away the shapeless dead;
Indra's foe, bereft of breath,
Slept the endless sleep of death!

Indra is the god of the morning light as well as of rain

11

Light was prisoned in the gloom,
Indra freed her from its womb;
Rain was prisoned in the cloud,
Indra smote the demon proud;
Oped the caverns of the night,
Gave us rain and gave us light!

12

Vain were Vritra's angry blows,
Indra shielded him from foes;
And he freed the captive kine,
Conquered Soma's sparkling wine,
Rolled seven rivers famed of old,
Feeding nations as they rolled!

13

Bolt of thunder, storm of hail,
'Gainst the hero harmless fell;
Shrouds of mists and gusts of rain
'Gainst the scatheless God were vain;
Vritra strove in furious mood,
Calm the conquering Indra stood!

14

Indra! When thy foe was dead,
Didst thou dimly, darkly dread
Some avenger in the fray;
Didst thou like a bird of prey
Swoop o'er ninety streams and nine
Through the blue sky which was thine?

15

Thunder armèd Sovran-king,
Of each life and lifeless thing,
Of each creature in his station,
Of each clime and race and nation!
Spokes are circled by the rim,
Worlds encircled live in *Him*!

Rig Veda, I. 32.

The God who gives rain to men is the God of the universe

II

INDRA, THE SUPREME GOD

1

HIGHEST of Immortals bright,
God of gods by lofty might,
He, before whose prowess high
Tremble earth and upper sky,
He is,—mortals, hear my verse,—
Indra, Lord of Universe!

2

He, who fixed the staggering earth,
Shaped the mountains at their birth,
Sky's blue vault held up and bent,
Measured out the firmament,
He is,—listen to my verse,—
Indra, Lord of Universe!

A reply to atheists

3

He, who quelled the cloud-fiend's might,
Rolled the seven great rivers bright,
Pierced the caverns of the gloom,
Conquered bright kine from its womb,
Lit the lightning's fire of old,
He is Indra, warrior bold!

4

He, who shaped with cunning hand
Wonders of the sea and land,
Quelled the Aryan's impious foe,
Doomed the Dasa to his woe,
Robbed the bandit in his hold,
He is Indra, hunter bold!

5

Have you, doubting, questioned me,—
Where is Indra, who is He?
Mortals, in your impious thought
Have you whispered,—He is not!
Jealous God! In vengeance dire
He can smite ye in his ire!

6

But his ceaseless mercies seek
High and lowly, strong and weak,
Priest who chants his sacred lays,
Worshipper who sings his praise,
Him who on the altar's flame,
Pours libations to his name!

7

His the kine and steeds of war,
Village home and battle car;
His right arm uplifts the sun,
Opes the ruddy gates of dawn;
His red bolt the dark cloud rends,
Grateful showers for mortals sends!

Indra is the God of battles, of light and of rain

8

Hosts advancing to the fray
Cry to him on battle's day;
And the strong man shouts his fame,
And the lowly lisps his name;
Warrior-chief on battle-car
Prays to Indra, God of war!

9

We but triumph by his blade,
Nations court his friendly aid;
Moveless hills that heavenward tower
Tremble at his mighty power;
And the world so vast and broad,
Images the mighty God!

10

Swift his weapons, red and dire,
To the impious speak his ire;
And his favours never rain
On the boastful and the vain;
And his red right hand can smite
Godless Dasas in the fight!

Indra smites the Non-Aryan chiefs and also the fiends of drought

11

For he slew Sambara bold,
Sheltered in his mountain hold,
In the fortieth autumn-tide;
Slew the dragon in his pride,
Vritra, rain-withholding cloud,
Titan of the inky shroud!

12

Seven bright rays bedeck his bow,
Seven great rivers from him flow;
Thunder-armèd, quick to ire,
He, in vengeance swift and dire,
Laid the proud Rauhina low,
Heaven-aspiring impious foe!

13

Earth and sky confess his sway,
Trembling hills obeisance pay;
Wielder of the bolt of heaven,
Be to him libations given;—
He accepts this Soma wine,
Listens to this lay of mine!

14

Brew the Soma fresh and fair,
Pour libations rich and rare,
For he blesses when we pray,
Helps the singer of his lay;—
He accepts this Soma wine,
Listens to this lay of mine!

15

Libations of the juice of Soma

Mighty Indra, strong and true,
Hymns to thee and gifts are due,
And our priests libations pour
For thy blessings' endless store;
Speak to us,—for thou art near,—
Let our brave sons know no fear!

Rig Veda, II. 12.

III

VARUNA, GOD OF LAW

In the dim and misty past, before the Indo-Aryans and the Iranians separated, Varuna was the highest and holiest of the Gods of their ancestors, and represented the spiritual side of their religion. After the separation had taken place, this deity of righteousness was translated in Iran into Ahura Mazd, the Supreme Deity. And in India too, Varuna never became divested of that sanctity and holiness which entered into his first conception, and the holiest hymns of the Rig Veda are his, not Indra's. In Greece he was called Uranos.

1

WHAT Immortal wakes my song,
Unto whom my lays belong?
Fair Aditi! Shine before us,
Mother of Light! To thee restore us,—
That my father I may see,
With my mother I may be!

Agni is the God of fire. Savitri is the rising sun. Surya is the sun of the day

2

Flame Immortal, Agni bright,
We invoke thy holy light!
Priest and God! He shines before us,
To Aditi shall restore us,—
That my father I may see,
With my mother I may be!

3

Bright Savitri, Sun unrisen,
Beam upon our earthly prison!
Thine is every golden treasure,
Grant to us our earthly measure,—
Grant, they never may grow less,
Hope and health and happiness!

4

Golden-handed God of Light,
Grant thy stainless favours bright,
May thy gifts upon us wait
Free from sin, reproach, and hate,—
Grant they never may grow less,
Hope and health and happiness!

5

Life-inspiring God of Day,
Mortals for thy favours pray,
Thou hast wealth for sons of men
Affluence beyond their ken,—
Radiant Bhaga deals thy grace,
Hope and health and happiness!

6

Lord Varuna, Righteous King,
Joyous heavens thy glories sing;
Not the birds that sail the sky
Thy resistless speed can vie,
Not the winds in ceaseless course
Nor the torrent's matchless force!

Varuna is the God of sky,—afterwards the God of oceans and all waters

7

Lord Varuna, Hallowed Light,
Throned in Heaven's etherial height,
Thine the radiance, rooted high,
Streaming downwards from the sky;
May it fill our heart with gladness
Quell the gloom of sin and sadness!

8

Thine the mighty hand hath laid,
Pathway for the sun to tread,
Thine the finger, day to day
Points to him his viewless way,
Thine the rays that darkness banish,
Sorrow, sin, and sadness vanish!

9

Hundred thousand balms that heal
From thy hands on mortals steal;
Hundred thousand blessings pour
From thy mercy's endless store;
Teach us, future sins to shun,
Save us, Lord, from sins we've done!

The Great Bear constellation

10

Yonder radiant stars of night,
Where are they when dawns the light?
Nature owns thy changeless law,
Universe obeys in awe,
And the orb of silver ray
Silent walks her nightly way!

11

Teach me, Lord, to chant thy lays,
And with gifts repeat thy praise;
Stay with us devoid of wrath,
Save us from the downward path;
World-extending in thy might,
Ruler of the realms of light!

12

Sages tell me night and day,
And my whispering heart doth say:—
Let the sinner in his chains
Ask his grace who grace ordains;
He is King and he is Love,
Bonds of sin he can remove!

13

Shackled to the three-fold stake,
Suppliant for his grace, I speak:—
May Aditi's Royal Son
Heed this humble worship done,
May he who in mercy reigns
Loose the fettered captive's chains!

14

Loose the fetters from above,
Mid and lower chains remove;
Free from sins, in law abiding,
May we heed thy holy guiding;
Stand, Aditi's Son, before us,
To Aditi yet restore us!

Varuna, son of Aditi, frees the captive fettered to the stake

Rig Veda, I. 24.

IV

VARUNA, GOD OF MERCY

1

Nations laud his works of wonder
Earth and sky who parts asunder,
Heaven's blue vault who holds on high,
Lights the star-lamps in the sky,
And the ocean-girdled land
Shapeth with a cunning hand!

2

King Varuna, throned aloft!
In my heart I question oft:—
Can a humble man unite
With the Lord of righteous might;—
Can a mortal win thy grace
View thy mercy-beaming face?

Varuna in his wrath smites the sinner

3

Unto seer and sage I turn,
Question oft that I may learn :—
What dark sin pollutes my heart,
What sweet balm will heal the smart ;—
Sages tell :—Varuna's wrath
Flings a shadow on my path !

4

Teach me, Lord, what crime unknown
Hath its shadows on me thrown ;
Wherefore in thy anger slay
Worshipper who sings thy lay?
Nay, from sin and passion free,
Teach me, Lord, to turn to thee !

5

Bid me expiate and shun
Follies by my fathers done ;
Make me fetterless and freed
From my own unholy deed ;
Chained like beast or trembling thief,
From thee, Lord, I seek relief !

6

Pride and passion oft betray,
Dice and drinking lead astray ;
Not our will but thoughlessness
Leads to danger and distress,
Elders oft the young will lead,
Even our dreams will passions breed !

7

Varuna pardons the repentant sinner

Let me, then, from passions free,
As thy bond-slave come to thee;
Thou canst grant unto the lowly
Gift of grace and wisdom holy;
Thou canst lead the wise and great
To the blest and happy state!

8

May this humble worship done,
Lord Varuna, reach thy throne;
May this simple lay of love,
King of skies, thy spirit move;
In our rest, and in our labour,
Tend us still with constant favour!

Rig Veda, VII. 86.

V

SAVITRI, THE SUN-GOD

Surya and Savitri are the most common names of the sun in the Rig Veda, the former word answering to the Greek Helios, the Latin Sol, and the Iranian Khorshed. Commentators draw a distinction between Savitri, the rising or the unrisen sun, and Surya, the bright sun of the day.

1

BRIGHT Savitri wakes my song,
Morning lays to him belong;—

Savitri is the rising sun

For he brings to sons of men
Corn and kine and wealth of grain;—
May he send his blessings fair,
Gifts and favours rich and rare!

2

Shining One! To Gods in heaven
Life immortal thou hast given,—
Unto men upon the earth
Granted mortals' humbler birth,—
Ray of life succeeding ray
As the day succeedeth day!

3

Spirit of the rising sun!
Deeds of darkness we have done,
And to pride and passion given
Sinned against the Gods in heaven;
Make us sinless of each stain,
Pure in sight of Gods and men!

4

All-pervading Lord of Light,
Universe-embracing Might!
From thy rosy hands are given
Tints on earth and lights in heaven;
Fixed thy law, thy purpose sure,
And thy mighty works endure!

5

On each lofty hill and glade
Home for Bright Ones thou hast made,

In the green and fertile vale
Mortals by thy mandate dwell,
Gods and men thy power attest,
Universe obeys thy hest!

He has fixed the homes of gods and men

6

Rich libations thrice we pour
For thy favours' endless store;
Mighty Indra, Earth and Sky,
Śindhu's streams that seaward hie,
Sons of Aditi the blest,
Grant us shelter, peace, and rest!

Rig Veda, IV. 54.

VI

USHAS, THE DAWN-GODDESS

There is no lovelier conception in the Rig Veda than that of the Dawn. There are no hymns in the Veda more truly poetical than those dedicated to her, and nothing more charming is to be found in the lyrical poetry of any ancient nation. The Dawn was known in the misty past ages by various names, and most of these names, and the legends connected with them, were brought by the Hindus from their original abode, since we find phonetical equivalents of these names, and a repetition of some of the legends too, in Greek mythology. Ushas is the Eos of the Greeks and the Aurora of the Latins. Arjuni, according to philologists, is the Greek Argynoris, Brisaya is Briseis, and Dahana is Daphne. Saranyu, the mother of the Asvins, is the Greek Erinys, and Ahana is the renowned goddess Athena.

The Dawn is the white-robed daughter of the sky

1

USHAS! Daughter of the sky,
Hold thy ruddy lights on high;
Bring as food with dawning day,
Riches with thy radiant ray;
White-robed nymph of morning sky,
Bring us light, let shadows fly!

2

Rich in cattle, rich in steed,
With thy gifts to mortals speed;
Joyous nations hail thy name,
For thy favours chant thy fame;
Waken sounds of life and joy,
Grant us bliss without alloy!

3

Our fathers hailed thy crimson light,
As we hail thee, Goddess bright;
Ride thy sky-borne chariot brave
Like a ship on ocean wave;
Bring upon thy radiant car,
Light and lustre from afar!

4

Men of wisdom raise their song,
Morning hymns to thee belong;
Ancient Kanwa lifts his lay
To thy red resplendent ray,—
Kanwa wise in prophet's lore
Blesses those who feed the poor!

The Dawn rouses every one to his work like a careful housewife

5

Come like house-wife gentle-hearted,
Tending us, for night's departed,
Rousing with thy radiant ray,
Sending us to work of day;—
Men to various tasks repair,
Birds with wild notes fill the air!

6

To the strong their work you send,
To the weak your favours lend,
Be a house-wife unto all,
Waking nature hears your call;—
Men to various tasks repair,
Birds with wild notes fill the air!

7

Lo, she comes in crimson car,
Scattering splendour from afar;
From the realms beyond the sun
In her chariot comes the Dawn;
Ushas in her loveliness
Comes to rouse us and to bless!

8

Mortals in devotion bend,
Hymns and songs of joy ascend;
Ushas in her radiant beauty
Comes to wake us to our duty;
Brings us blessings in her car,
Drives all evil things afar!

The Dawn drives away the shades of night

9

White-robed daughter of the sky,
Hold thy ruddy light on high,
Day by day with dawning light
Bring us blessings ever bright,
Bring us blessings in thy car,
Drive the shades of night afar!

10

Golden nymph of grace divine,
Gift of life and light is thine,
Chase the shadows of the night,
Dawn in radiance red and bright,
Bring us blessings in thy car,
List unto our lay from far!

11

Win the vigour of the strong,
Manhood which to us belong;
Hark the lays to thee ascending
From our priests by altars bending;
Grant, our rites from harm be free,
And our hearts may turn to thee!

12

Come with dwellers of the sky,
Swift to our libations hie;
Grant us kine and warlike steed,
And our rites with blessings speed;
Grant us food and warrior's name,
Manhood's strength and soldier's fame!

The Dawn brings gifts and blessings to men

13

Maiden of the morning sky,
Fling thy radiance far and nigh;
Bear us riches in thy arm,
Shield us from each earthly harm;
Speed our crops and corn and grain,
Every gift which men attain!

14

Damsel of the dawning light,
Fathers hailed thy radiance bright,
Raised their voices in thy praise
Sang thy bounty in their lays;
We too chant thy deathless song,
And the ancient rites prolong!

15

Ope the portals of the sky,
Light comes in, let shadows fly;
Grant us happy homes and bright,
Free from discord, free from spite,
Milch-kine with their copious yield,
Wealth of crops from grateful field!

16

Bring us, nymph of loveliness,
Food to comfort and to bless,
Wealth and cattle rich and rare,
Joy and blessings fresh and fair;
Ushas! World-pervading Glory,
Mortals chant thy wonders story!

Rig Veda, I. 48.

VII

AGNI, GOD OF FIRE

"Agni is God of Fire; the Ignis of the Latins, the Ogni of the Sclavonians."—Muir's *Sanscrit Texts*.

"All the names of the Fire and the Fire-gods were carried away by the Western Aryans; and we have Prometheus answering to Pramantha, Phoronus to Bharanyu, and the Latin Vulcanus to the Sanscrit Ulka."—Cox's *Mythology of Aryan Nations*.

The poet of this hymn is Viswavara, a cultured woman

1

LIGHTED Agni flames forth high,
Flings a radiance on the sky,
And his lustre red and bright
Mingles with the morning light;
Facing east, with gifts and lays
Viswavara sings his praise!

2

First Immortal of the skies,
Minister of our sacrifice,
Unto him thy gifts prolong
Who uplifts thy sacred song,
Unto him thy blessings come
On whose altar is thy home!

3

Radiant on the altar shine,
Strength and lustre bright be thine;

Spread our riches with thy flame,
Quell our foemen's power and fame,
Bless our dwellings from above,
Men and women link in love!

As a woman, the poet prays for domestic happiness and love

4

Radiant on the altar shine,
Strength and lustre bright be thine;
Viswavara humbly bending
Chants thy glories never ending;
Form of splendour bright is thine,
On her altar ever shine!

5

Pious hands awake thy flame,
Pious lips repeat thy name;
Bear unto our sacrifice
Bright Immortals from the skies,
Bear unto the Gods in heaven
Sacred offerings to thee given!

6

Pious lips the chant uplift,
Pious hands provide the gift,
Priest of Gods, Immortal bright,
Thine is morning's sacred rite,
Messenger of Gods in heaven,
Take these offerings humbly given!

Rig Veda, V. 28

VIII

KSHETRA-PATI, GOD OF AGRICULTURE

Kshetra-pati means the God of the field

1

KSHETRA-PATI, Tiller's God,
Master of the grateful sod,
We will till the fruitful field,
With Him win its copious yield;
Strong our bullocks and our steeds,
He provides the tiller's needs!

2

Copious milk our cows supply,
Copious showers the helping sky,
Kshetra-pati sends his rain
To the toilers of the plain;
Lo! Our fields are broad and spacious,
Be the God of tillage gracious!

3

May our crops in sweetness grow,
And in sweetness waters flow,
Sweetly blow the perfumed air,
And the skies be bright and fair;
Thee we follow, Lord of might,
Be our harvest free from blight!

4

Song of tilling the earth

Gladly works the merry swain,
Glad the patient bullocks strain,
Merry o'er the yielding soil
Ploughshare marks the tiller's toil;
Fasten then the traces strong,
Ply the goad and move along!

5

Suna, Sira,—Plough and Share,—
Listen to the peasant's prayer;
Milk of rain from breast of heaven
Unto thirsty earth be given;
Store of waters feed the soil
And reward the peasant's toil!

6

Furrow, of the ploughshare born,—
Sita, bearing golden corn,—
Thee the toiling nations praise,
Listen to their grateful lays;
Be our meadows fed with rain,
Be our cornfields rich in grain!

7

Indra takes her by the hand,
Pushan leads her o'er the land,
From the sky obedient drops
At her bidding feed the crops;
Comes the harvest year by year,
Sita comes to help and cheer!

A song of pasture

8

Glad the ploughshare marks the plain,
Merrily toil the beasts and men,
And Parjanya, bounteous God,
Sends his showers to feed the sod;
To the Plough and Ploughshare sing,
Crops and fruitage they will bring!

Rig Veda, IV. 57.

IX

PUSHAN, GOD OF PASTURE

1

PUSHAN, God of golden day,
Shorten thou the shepherd's way,
Vanquish every foe and stranger,
Free our path from every danger;
Cloud-born Pushan, ever more,
Lead us as you led before!

2

Smite the wild wolf, fierce and vile,
Lurking in the dark defile,
Smite the robber and the thief,
Stealing forth to take our life;
Cloud-born Pushan, ever more,
Lead us as you led before!

3

Pushan protects travellers from harm

Chase him, Pushan, in thy wrath,
Who infests the lonely path,
Robber with his ruthless heart,
Slayer with his secret dart;
Child of clouds, for ever more,
Lead us as you led before!

4

Trample with thy heavy tread,
On the darksome man of dread,
On the low and lying knave,
Smooth-tongued double-dealing slave;
Child of clouds, for ever more,
Lead us as you led before!

5

Thou dost pathless forests know,
Thou canst quell the secret foe,
Thou didst lead our fathers right,
Wonder-worker, orb of light;
Grant from thy unfailing store
Wealth and blessings ever more!

6

Thou hast treasures manifold,
Glittering weapons, arms of gold;
Foremost of the Sons of Light,
Shepherds' God and Leader bright;
Grant from thy unfailing store
Wealth and blessings ever more!

Pushan leads shepherds to fresh pastures

7

Lead us through the dark defile
Past pursuers dread and vile,
Lead us over pleasant ways
Sheltered by thy saving grace,
Lead us o'er this trackless shore,
And we follow ever more!

8

Where the grass is rich and green,
And the pasture's beauteous seen,
And the meadow's soft and sweet,
Lead us, safe from scorching heat,
Blessings on thy servants pour,
And we follow ever more!

9

Fill our hearts with hope and courage,
Fill our homes with food and forage,
Save us from a cruel fate
Feed us and invigorate;
We are suppliants at thy door,
And we follow ever more!

10

Heart and voice we lift in praise,
Chant our hymns and pious lays,
From the Bright One, good and gracious,
Ask for food and pasture spaceous;
Shepherds' God! Befriend the poor,
And we follow ever more!

Rig Veda, I. 24.

X

A BATTLE HYMN

Sudas was an Aryan king and conqueror, and we are frequently told that ten Aryan tribes and kings combined against him, and he was victorious over them all. The allusions to these internecine wars among Aryan races, and to the particular tribes who fought against Sudas, are historically among the most important passages in the Rig Veda. The poet Tritsu or Vasishtha, who sang these deeds of Sudas's glory, was not unrewarded for his immortal verse. For in verses 22 and 23 (Hymn VII. 18) he acknowledges with gratitude that the valiant Sudas rewarded him with two hundred cows and two chariots and four horses with gold trappings.

1

Varuna and Indra invoked to protect King Sudas against invaders from the west

VARUNA, Indra, Gods of battle!
Foemen came for spoil and cattle,
Battle-axes in their hand,
Eastward came the armed band;—
By your grace Sudas arose,
Smote the dark and Aryan foes!

2

Gathered nations lifted high
Banners floating in the sky,
Warriors turned their anxious gaze
From the earth to sky's dark haze;—
None but you, our help and stay,
Saved Sudas on that dark day!

A vivid account of the battle-field

3

To the dazed, bewildered eye
Broad earth mingled with the sky,
And the deafening shout arose
From our men and circling foes;—
You then heard our priestly call,
Helped Sudas to conquer all!

4

Banded nations ye have quelled,
Bheda in the battle felled,
Ye were king Sudas's stay,
Saved him in the dubious fray;—
For ye heard our holy lay,
Tritsus' service won the day!

5

Wily was the foeman's heart,
And resistless was his dart;
Ye are Lords of earth and heaven,
To our king your aid was given;—
For ye heard our holy lay
Tritsus' prayers won the day!

6

Foemen called on you in vain,
For ye hear not impious men;
Foemen longed in vain for lands,
Impious hearts make feeble hands;
Ten great kings their warriors brought,—
You beside our monarch fought!

7

Jealousy between the Viswamitras and the Vasishthas

Ten great kings who knew no rite
Vainly did their troops unite,
And their useless weapons bring,
For they conquered not our king;
Fruitful was our warriors' boast,
And ye helped our conquering host!

8

With their long and braided hair
White-robed Tritsu priests appear,
And with hymn and holy song
Sacrificial rites prolong;
Gods have heard! Against the ten,
They have helped our king and men!

9

Indra rends the cloud's dark folds,
King Varuna law upholds,
To their glory, in their praise
Tritsus chant their pious lays;
Grant us, Lords, your sweet protection,
Blessings rich and benediction!

10

King Varuna, Indra strong,
Listen to the Tritsus' song;
Aryaman and Mitra bright,
Grant us shelter, Sons of Light;
Fair Aditi, primal ray,
Bright Savitri hear this lay!

Rig Veda, VII. 83.

XI

THE ALL-CREATOR

The All-Creator

1

Our Father at creation's birth
Made the sky and vasty earth,
When commingled earth and sky
In a watery form did lie;
He made fast and firm the land,
Stretched the sky-vault by His hand!

2

All-Creator! His Creation
Is each being in his station;
All-disposer! High in grace,
Higher than the stars his place;
All-sustainer! Worship done
By the sages reach the One!

3

He the Father,—made us all,
He the Ruler,—hears our call,
He the Feeder,—feeds each nation,
Every creature in its station;
Names of many Gods He bears,
He is One,—we seek by prayers!

4

Him they offered rites of old,
Rishis holy, prophets bold;

The one true God

Him they praised in sacred song,
Worshippers a pious throng;
Him they call from diverse places
Who hath shaped all things and races!

5

Ere was born the heaven or earth,
Gods or Titans sprang to birth,
What was it,—primeval, lone,—
Germ that in the waters shone?
Who at dim creation's morn
Placed the Germ whence Gods were born?

6

Unborn gods commingled lived
In the Germ the floods received,
In the navel of the *One*
Lived the Germ, primeval, lone;
From the Uncreate have sprung
Creatures that to Him belong!

7

Him ye do not comprehend,—
Nature's Cause, Creation's End;
Him ye see but wrapped in gloom,—
Who is Life and final Doom;
Priests and chanters of the lay
Listless wander from the way!

Rig Veda, X. 82.

XII

THE GOLDEN CHILD

The Golden Child

I

To what God in earth or air
Shall we offer gift and prayer?
Him,—the Golden Child,—the One,
Lord of all since nature's dawn;
Ocean-compassed earth He spread,
Flung the sky-vault overhead!

2

To what God in earth or air
Shall we offer gift and prayer?
Him who lit life's primal ray,
And whom heavenly hosts obey,
Him whose darkening shade is Death,
And whose light—Immortal Breath!

3

To what God in earth or air
Shall we offer gift and prayer?
Him,—the Ruler-king above
Of all things that live and move,
Him who formed the beast and man
When creation's life began!

4

He is the Creator, Ruler of all

To what God in earth or air
Shall we offer gift and prayer?
Him whose mighty hand hath made
Snowy mountains, ocean's bed,
Whose vast arms—the spreading sky,
Far-extending, flaming high!

5

To what God in earth or air
Shall we offer gift and prayer?
Him who fixed the earth and sky,
Starry heavens suspended high,
And the blue-vault shaped and bent,
Measured out the firmament!

6

To what God in earth or air
Shall we offer gift and prayer?
Him whom earth and sounding sky
Render worship pure and high,
And the sun each circling hour
Borrows radiance from His power?

7

To what God in earth or air
Shall we offer gift and prayer?
Him, the Life of Gods, the ONE,
Rising at creation's dawn,
When deep waters held in gloom
Unborn Agni in their womb!

8

Agni or fire, *i.e.* cosmic energy

To what God in earth or air
Shall we offer gift and prayer?
Him, the God of Gods,—the ONE,—
Who o'er primal waters shone,
When the deep brought forth in gloom
Nascent Agni from her womb.

9

To what God in earth or air
Shall we offer gift and prayer?
Him, the vasty earth who made,
Nature's changeless laws who laid,
Rolled the great and lucid floods,
World's creator, God of Gods!

10

Lord of creatures! Thou dost know
Things created here below;
Thou above canst comprehend
Vast creation's cause and end;
Grant us blessing and protection,
Grant us wealth and benediction!

Rig Veda, X. 121.

II

PASSAGES FROM THE UPANISHADS

Date, Circa 1000 *B.C.*

"From every sentence, deep, original, and sublime thoughts arise, and the whole is pervaded by a high and holy and earnest spirit. Indian air surrounds us, and original thoughts of kindred spirits. . . . In the whole world there is no study except that of the originals, so beneficial and so elevating as that of the Oupnekhat. It has been the solace of my life; it will be the solace of my death."—*Schopenhauer.*

I

THE UNIVERSAL SOUL

1

ALL this universe is BRAHMA,—
All that live and move and die,—
Born in Him, in Him subsisting,
Ending in that Being High.
And the mortal ever reapeth
As he sows upon this earth,
As he lives in sin or virtue
So he takes his future birth!

The Deity is the Cosmos, —all that exists is a part of Him

2

He is Life and highest Knowledge,
He is Truth and holy Light,
And his soul the world pervadeth
But like ether 'scapes our sight.
From Him every deed and action,
Every wish and impulse spring,
Calm and conscious, never speaking,
He embraceth everything!

3

He—the self within my bosom,
Impulse of the heart and brain,

He is in every creature and comprises the universe

Smaller than the smallest substance,
Kernel of the smallest grain.
He—the self within my bosom,
Greater than the earth and sky,
Vaster than the lands and oceans,
Higher than the heaven on high!

4

From Him every deed and action,
Every wish and impulse spring,
Calm and conscious, never speaking,
He embraceth everything.
He the self within my bosom,
He the universal goal,—
When I leave this world of mortals
Unto Him will wing my soul!

Chhandogya Upanishad.

II

THE LEGEND OF SATYAKAMA

1

SATYAKAMA, truth-beloving,
Whom the poor Jabala bore,
Felt a longing love for knowledge,
Hidden truth and highest lore.
And he came unto his mother,
Asked her of his father's name,—
"Mother, I would be a student,
Tell me from what line I came."

Jabala, born in shame, dares to be a seeker of the truth

2

Poor Jabala, erring woman,
    Spake in shame but spake the truth,—
"Sinfully I lived and wandered,
    And I bore thee in my youth.
And I know not of thy father,
    Know not of what line thou art,
Take thy surname from thy mother,
    Offspring of her erring heart."

3

Humbled by the sad recital
    To Gautama went the youth,—
"I would be a student, Father,
    For I wish to know the truth."
Gautama with kindly greetings
    Asked the student whence he came,—
"Tell me of what line thou comest,
    Tell me what may be thy name."

4

Satyakama, truth-beloving,
    Spake in shame but spake the truth,—
"Sinfully my mother wandered,
    And she bore me in her youth;
Scarce I know who be my father,
    Scarcely, of what line I came,
Poor Jabala is my mother,
    And Jabala be my name."

Truth makes a Brahman

5

"Hold, my friend and faithful student,"—
Spake the sage unto the youth,
"By thy worth thou art a Brahman
For thou darest speak the truth.
Go and fetch the sacred fuel,
I will teach thee lessons high,
Sacred learning of our fathers,
For thy accents shaped no lie!"

6

Satyakama brought the fuel,
Was a student young and brave,
And he kept his teacher's cattle,
Served his teacher as his slave.
And in field and pathless jungle
Still he pondered as he went,
Nature to his eager question
Helping light and guidance lent.

7

From the bull so strong and sturdy
Of the herd he tended well,
From the red and flaming faggot
Lighted when the evening fell,
From the gay and bright flamingo
As it sailed across the sky,
From the diver-bird so beauteous
Clad in plumes of rainbow dye,

8

All nature has lessons for him who seeks the truth

From the thoughts that rose within him
When he sat without a friend,
When the evening fire he lighted
And the cattle he had penned,
From each high and humble object
Came its meaning to the youth,
From the secret lamp of Nature
Flashed on him the light of Truth!

9

And he came to sage Gautama
With a bright and beaming face,—
Sacred truth and holy wisdom
Brings its gladness and its grace.
"Lo! a light is on thy forehead,
Dost thou then of BRAHMA know?
Only those who know the True One
With such inward gladness glow!"

10

"Father, I have sought to fathom,"—
Softly answered thus the youth,—
"From the objects of creation,
Not from man, the highest truth.
Boundless space and vault of azure,
Sky and earth and ocean broad,
Sun and moon and soul immortal,—
All is BRAHMA, all is GOD!"

Abridged from the Chhandogya Upanishad.

III

THE LEGEND OF GARGI

Videha is North Behar, Kuruland is Delhi district, and Panchala is the country about Kanoug

1

JANAK, bold and bounteous monarch,
Erst in broad Videha reigned,
Held his rites in regal splendour
And an ample feast ordained.
Brahmans from the Kuru kingdom
And from fair Panchala came,
For they knew of Janak's bounty
And they heard of Janak's fame.

2

Who of these assembled Brahmans,
To the sacrifice who came,
Was the deepest versed in Vedas,
Worthiest of a Brahman's name?
Thus a question stirred the bosom
Of the monarch proud and bold,
And he penned a thousand milch kine,
On each horn was hung some gold.

3

"Saintly teachers, learned Brahmans,
Welcome to my royal feast,
Let him win a thousand milch kine
Who is wisest and the best,

Contests among the learned

Who is deepest in his learning,
    Let him stand and win the gold?"
Thus to teachers of the Vedas
    Spake the monarch calm and bold.

4

Brahmans heard the royal mandate,
    Durst not stand and win the prize,—
Where so many wise men gathered
    Who could claim to be most wise?
Up stood learned Yajna-valkya,—
    Janak's proud preceptor he,—
And the priest spake to his pupil,
    "Drive the cattle home for me!"

5

Wrathful were the other Brahmans,—
    Asvala, invoking priest,
Arta-bhaga, versed in Vedas,
    Lahya-yani, lord of feast,
Chakra-yana, Kaushi-taki,
    Udda-laka stood before,
And with questions deep contested
    Yajna-valkya's Vedic lore!

6

Yajna-valkya, proud and peerless,
    Answered them with priestly pride,
As a towering moveless mountain
    Beateth back the ocean's tide.

Gargi's first question

Then stood sage and saintly Gargi,
Dark locks graced her woman's head,
Wise was she as wisest Brahman,
Learned as the deepest-read!

7

"As a chief of Kasi's kingdom,
Or Videha's warlike land,
Lifts his bow to face the battle,
Takes his arrows in his hand,
Even so, great Yajna-valkya,
I will rise to challange thee,
Ask thee, priest, to face my questions,
List to them and answer me!

8

"On the broad earth far extending,
In the firmament and sky,
In the present, past, and future,
Ever living, ever nigh,
In the wide space interwoven
Like the warp and like the woof,
What pervades, unseen, unfathomed,
Earth below and heaven's high roof?"

9

"Subtle question, saintly Gargi,
Deep enquiry hast thou made,—
But 'tis ether, viewless, shapeless,
Which doth earth and sky pervade."

Her second question

"Subtle answer, Yajna-valkya,
In thy wisdom thou hast given,—
But what is this viewless ether,
Wherein is it interwoven?"

10

"Deeper, Gargi, is this question,—
Wherein is the ether woven,
Wherein dwell the past and future
Wherein rest the earth and heaven?
'Tis the uncreate IMMORTAL,
Viewless,—fills the world so broad,
Flameless,—burns not like the red fire,
Moveless,—sweeps not like the flood!

11

"Without shadow, without darkness,
He is neither air nor sky,
Void of taste and touch and feeling
He subsists sublime and high!
Without hearing—hears all nature,
Views creation—void of sight,
Void of limbs—but ever acting,
Void of form—but Infinite!

12

"Gargi, wouldst thou further fathom?
He ordains the night and day,
Earth and sky confess His mandate,
Sun and moon his hests obey!

The Deity is interwoven in all nature

He hath shaped the seas and mountains,
Life to creatures he hath given,
Darkly-acting, dimly present,
In all Nature interwoven!"

Abridged from the Brihad-aranyaka Upanishad.

IV

THE LEGEND OF MAITREYI

I

Unto her, his well-beloved,—
Maitreyi his pious wife,—
Spake the saintly Yajna-valkya,
When he took to forest life.
"Worldly wealth and every object
Now I leave behind, my fair,
Katyayani takes her portion,
Thou, Maitreyi, take thy share."

2

"Worldly wealth and precious objects,"
Asked the pious-hearted wife,
"Will they lead to my salvation,
Lead me to immortal life?"
"Nay, they lead not to salvation,
Lead not to a higher state,
But the life the rich man liveth
Shall be, dear-loved wife, thy fate."

Maitreyi despises wealth and seeks the truth

3

" But the life the rich man liveth
    Unto me, my lord, were vain,
Teach me that which works salvation,
    Life immortal I would gain."
" Ever dear, my sweet Maitreyi,
    Dearer now art thou to me,
And the wealth that works salvation,
    I will leave that wealth to thee!

4

" Love of man and faithful woman,
    Ties that friends with friends combine,
Love of parents and of children,
    Tendance of our flocks and kine,
Love of every outward object
    Of our inner love is part,—
Love thy self, and all creation
    Claims a portion of thy heart!

5

" Sound the drum, a music issues,
    Can you grasp the sound so bold?
Blow the conch at festive season,
    Can you that soft utterance hold?
Strike the harp-string deep-resounding,
    Can you touch its voice profound?
Stop the drum, the conch, the harp string,
    And you stop the uttered sound!

6

Every soul is a part of the universal soul

"Thus through self within your bosom
Outer nature you control,
For your self is kin to nature,
Portion of the Mighty Soul.
From the fire a deep cloud issues,
Various-shaped it floats on high,
From the Mighty Soul thus issue
Forms that people earth and sky!

7

"He breathed forth the vast creation,
Vedas, Sastras, all are His,
Sense and sight and self within us,
Worlds and mountains and the seas.
He is like the tintless crystal,
Shapeless, viewless, dark and dim,
Spring from Him all shapes in nature,
All the worlds will merge in Him!"

8

"But my love!" exclaimed Maitreyi,
"Pardon if I somewhat fail,—
Weak is woman's sense and reason,
And obscure the truth you tell."
"Not so," Yajna-valkya answered,
"Know a part, you grasp the whole,
Clear as is the sun at midday
Is the Universal Soul!

9

The universal soul is unseen but omnipresent

" All the outer worlds pervading,
And the orbs that ceaseless roll,
All the cosmic force directing,
Is—the Universal Soul.
All unseen, but manifested
In the sky and earth so broad,
All-surveying, ever present,—
He is BRAHMA, He is GOD ! "

Abridged from Bribad-aranyaka Upanishad.

V

THE LEGEND OF BALAKI

I

Bold Balaki was a Brahman
Proud of learning and of lore,
Versed in Veda and in Sastra,
Known in many a distant shore,
In the realm of Usinara
And in Matsya he had been,
Kuruland and broad Panchala,
Kasi and Videha seen.

2

Royal sage Ajata-satru
Ruled in Kasi rich in fame,
Unto him the learned Brahman
As a guest and stranger came.

The Brahman professes to teach

"Blessed be thy rule, O monarch,
And thy empire rich and fair,
I will speak to thee of BRAHMA,
Ruler of the earth and air!"

3

"Welcome, welcome, learned Brahman,
Handsome be thy learning's meed,
For thy holy speech I offer
Thousand kine of finest breed.
All the priests and sages hasten
To Videha's mightier king,
Come thou to the court of Kasi
And a Brahman's blessings bring!"

4

"Listen, then, O pious monarch,
Mark the sun so fair and bright,
Worship thou the Soul of Radiance
Dwelling in that orb of light!"
"Higher message, priest Balaki,
Deeper lesson must thou state,
For the sun is great and glorious,
But is not the Uncreate!"

5

"Mark the moon, O mighty monarch,
Sailing o'er the silent sky,
Worship thou the Soul of Beauty
Dwelling there serene and high!"

"Higher message, priest Balaki,
Deeper lesson must thou state,
For the moon is bright and beauteous,
But is not the Uncreate!" But the King is not satisfied

6

"Mark, O king, the forked lightning
Leaping through the lurid sky,
Worship thou the Soul of Terror
Flashing there sublime and high!"
"Higher message, priest Balaki,
Deeper lesson must thou state,
For the lightning is terrific,
But is not the Uncreate!"

7

"List, O king, in voice of thunder
Mandate high and law profound,
Worship thou the Soul of Grandeur
Dwelling in that lofty sound!"
"Higher message, priest Balaki,
Deeper lesson thou must state,
Mighty is the peal of thunder,
But is not the Uncreate!"

8

Laboured still the learned Brahman
Nature's secrets to explain,
Quoted from each holy Sastra,
Argued long, but argued vain,

The Brahman fails to teach, and seeks to learn

To his reasons, to his learning,
    Simply this the monarch said:
Glorious is this wide creation,—
    Uncreate the hand that made!

9

Scroll and scripture and tradition,
    Proud Balaki quoted oft,
Spoke of fire and viewless ether,
    Seas below and skies aloft,
Spoke of shadow and reflection,
    Word and echo, voice and sound,
Argued still of dream and slumber,
    But solution none he found!

10

Silent was the boastful Brahman,
    Bent his humbled head in shame,
Sad at heart in pride of wisdom
    To a wiser king he came.
"Thus far,"—spake the monarch gently,—
    "Thus far doth your knowledge go?"
"Thus far,"—spake the Brahman humbly,—
    "Teach me what you further know?"

11

With the fuel, as a student,
    Meekly priest Balaki came,
Seeking knowledge from the monarch
    Great in wisdom as in fame.

"He the sun and moon who lighted,
Spread the earth and sky so great,
Hung the star-lamps in the azure,—
He alone is Uncreate!"

The King teaches the Brahman

Abridged from the Kaushitaki Upanishad.

VI

DEATH'S SECRET

1

Nich-ketas, young and living,
Sent to regions of the dead,
Questioned thus the mighty Yama,—
Death's deep secret he would read.—
"There is doubt, O sable monarch,
When an earthly mortal dies,
Is that death his final ending,
Doth he live again in skies?"

2

Answered him the sable monarch,—
Yama, ruler of the dead,—
"Mortals often ask that question,
Gods my secret may not read.
Not revealed to Gods or mortals
Is the mystery of death,
Ask for other boon and blessing,
Ask of creatures drawing breath.

The seeker after truth is put off

3

" Ask for sons and happy grandsons,
Who shall live a hundred years,
Gold and garments, cars and horses,
Life exempt from ills and fears.
Lord of broad and fertile acres,
Rich in fruitage, corn and wine,
Many autumns, as thou willest,
Life of happiness be thine!

4

" Higher hopes and aspirations
If thy noble heart doth frame,
Seek for prowess and for glory,
And a hero's deathless fame.
Be a king of spacious kingdoms,
Be a lord upon the earth,
Happy in thy life's fruition
Be the foremost in thy worth!

5

" Or if softer pleasures tempt thee,
Sweeter joys of earth be thine,
Lute and lyre and heavenly music,
Damsels fair and sparkling wine.
Be attended by these maidens,—
Such as these men do not see,—
Ask for every boon and favour,
Leave my secret unto me!"

6

But the seeker after truth will not be put off

"These are," Nachi-ketas answered,
"Pleasures that will pass away,
What will please us in the present
Fade to-morrow and decay.
Keep thy dance and heavenly music,
Maidens young and fresh as May,
Teach me thy great secret only,
Secret of the after-day!"

7

"To the pious," Yama answered,
"Is all mystery revealed,
To the man of contemplation
Life and Death their secret yield
And he sees the Soul Immortal
Darkly hid from mortal eyes,
Mutely feels the throbbing presence
Of the Lord of earth and skies!

8

And the man who knows this secret
Earthly cravings can control,
Passes from his earthly prison,
Mingles with the Mighty Soul.
Nachi-ketas, this my secret,—
BRAHMA is the Mighty Breath,
BRAHMA'S house is ever open,
Life existeth after death!"

Abridged from the Katha Upanishad

III

PASSAGES FROM BUDDHIST LITERATURE

Date 500 to 200 B.C.
The last piece selected is of later date.

"The *Three Pitakas* were composed, settled, and arranged in India during the hundred or two hundred years after the death of Gautama Buddha. The works comprised in the Sutta Pitaka profess to record the sayings and doings of Gautama Buddha himself. The Vinaya Pitaka contains very minute rules, often on the most trivial subjects, for the conduct of monks and nuns. And lastly, the Abhidhamma Pitaka contains disquisitions on various subjects, on the conditions of life in different worlds, on personal qualities, on the elements, on the causes of existence, &c."

Civilisation in Ancient India.

I

BUDDHA'S BIRTH

The Bright Gods hail the birth of Buddha

1

SAGE ASITA saw a vision,—
When our Master took His birth,—
Saw the Bright Gods all assembled,
Wafting blessings to the earth.
"Wherefore are the Bright Gods wafting
Salutations from the sky,
Flinging on the earth a radiance
From their concourse great and high?"
"Tis because the Lord and Master,
For the weary and the worn,
In the kingdom of the Sakyas
In Lumbini's grove is born!"

2

Sage Asita in his wisdom
Spake to Sakya's saintly king,—
"Unto thee a babe is given,
Gods to him their homage bring!"
And he saw the child of lustre,
Gold-like, wrought by cunning hand,
Beaming with an inward glory,
Jewel of the happy land.

The Sage foretells the mission of Buddha

"He is born our Lord and Master,"
So the sage Asita said,
"He shall be the Great Awakened,
And the rule of love shall spread."

3

And the blind received their vision,
So, the bright babe they might see,
And the deaf man heard a music,
Strains of peace and piety!
Hymns of praise the speechless uttered
To the Lord and Master come,
Lame and crooked, halt and stricken,
Ran rejoicing to their home!
Chains and shackles fell asunder
In the prisons of the earth,
Skies with brighter light and lustre
Hailed the Child's auspicious birth!

From the Nalaka Sutta & Birth Stories.

II

BUDDHA'S DEATH

I

Thus in many lands they wandered,
Buddha and his faithful friend,
Teaching truth to many nations,
Till his life approached its end.

And they say, along the pathway,
As the saintly Master went,
Fruit-trees blossomed out of season
And a lovely fragrance lent.
And that flowers and sandal-powder
Gently fell on him from high,
And that strains of heavenly music
Sounded from the sunlit sky!

Nature pays homage to Buddha

2

But the saintly Master whispered
To his friend beloved and blest,
"Tis not thus, O friend Ananda,
That the Buddha's honoured best.
Not by flowers or sandal-powder,
Not by music's heavenly strain,
Is the soul's true worship rendered,
Useless are these things and vain.
But the brother and the sister,
Man devout and woman holy,—
Pure in life, in duty faithful,—
They perform the worship truly!"

3

Night came on, and saintly Buddha
Slept in suffering, sick and wan,
When a Brahman, seeking wisdom,
Came to see the holy man.
Anxiously Ananda stopped him,
But spake Buddha, though in pain,
"He who comes to seek for wisdom
Shall not come to me in vain."

Love those who hate ye

And he to the pious stranger
    Told the truth in language plain,
Taught the law with dying accents,
    Stopped, and never spake again!

From the Mahaparinibbana Sutta.

III

BUDDHA'S PRECEPTS

1

Render hate to those who hate you,
    Deeper rolls the stream of strife;
Render love and healing kindness,
    Hatred dies and sweet is life!

2

Pious precepts, smooth-tongued preacher,
    Never acted, wisely meant,
Are like gay and golden blossoms
    Without fragrance, without scent!

3

Dost thou shrink from death and suffering,
    Dost thou cling to life from birth?
So doth every brother-creature,—
    Harm not living things on earth!

4

Forgive those who smite ye

Unto those who live in hatred
Thou shalt bear unchanging love,
Unto those who smite in anger
Thou shalt thy forgiveness prove !

5

Pious acts endure for ever,
And in heaven the doer meet,
As his loved and loving kinsmen
Home-returning kinsman greet !

6

By your Love the wrathful conquer,
By your Grace the ill pursue,
By your Charity the miser,
By your Truth the false subdue !

7

Faults of other men ye question,
Not the evil ye have done,
Neighbour's sins like chaff ye winnow,
Like a false die hide your own !

8

Not a sage and not an elder
Is the man advanced in age,
Truth and virtue, love and kindness,
Make the elder and the sage !

Outward penance is vain when there is ravening within

9

Not by skins and plaited tresses,
Not by family and birth,
But by truth and righteous conduct
Is the Brahman known on earth!

10

Wherefore then thy plaited tresses
And thy holy robe of skin,
What avails this outward penance
When there's ravening within?

From the Dhamma-pada.

IV

ASOKA'S MESSAGE TO HIS PEOPLE

Asoka the Great ruled India from 260 to 222 B.C., embraced the Buddhist religion, and spread it over India and far beyond the limits of India. "If a man's fame," says Kopen, "can be measured by the number of hearts who revere his memory, by the number of lips who have mentioned and still mention him with honour, Asoka is more famous than Charlemagne or Cæsar."

I

THUS spake royal Piyadasi,
Of the Gods beloved:
"Grace and righteous exhortation
Have my subjects moved,

For my pastors to the people
    Holy lessons sing,—
And my priests to countless thousands
    Loving message bring!

Religious instruction to the people

2

"I have spoke to subject peoples
    Precepts I have loved,
I have carved on rock-made pillars
    Lessons I have proved.
Ministers of faith and duty
    Have my mandates told,—
Spoke to near and distant nations
    Maxims loved of old!

3

"And within my spacious empire,
    By each highway made,
Figs and mangoes I have planted
    For repose and shade,
Wells I made for man and cattle,
    All that breathe and move,—
But with higher toil constructed
    Springs of faith and love!

4

"Scatter then my royal riches,
    Spread my bounty then,
To the monk and to the toiler,
    To all living men,

Gifts to the people without distinction

To the Brahman and the Sraman,
To all sects of fame,—
Let each clan and corporation
Know Asoka's name!

5

"And unto my royal bounty
Others add their store,
For my queens with queenly mercy
Help the helpless poor;
And my white-robed royal children
Acts of kindness prove,—
Charity and Truth and Kindness,
Purity and Love!

6

"Thus in ever growing current
May our bounty flow,
To the Brahman and the Sraman,
To the poor and low;
For the humble and the lowly
Special kindness crave,—
May our mercy reach the menial,
Cheer the unchained slave!

7

"Laws severe we vainly fashion,
Codes we vainly start,
Gentle teaching, soft persuasion,
Touch the people's heart.

Moral teachings and not codes touch the people's heart

Hence I carve this loving edict,
Speak these maxims pure,—
Future kings will work as long as
Sun and moon endure!

8

"Since I won my father's Empire,
Since this State was mine,
Past are seven and twenty autumns
When I carve this line.
Where 'tis writ on stony pillar
In this Empire vast,—
Unto far and distant ages
May this Edict last!"

Pillar Edict, VIII.

V

ASOKA'S MESSAGE TO FOREIGN NATIONS

I

KING and victor Piyadasi,
Of the Gods beloved,
O'er the plains of broad Kalinga
With his army moved.
Hundred thousand men were taken,
Hundred thousand died,—
Righteous sorrow wrung his bosom,
And the victor cried:

Evils attendant on war

2

" Brahmans pure and Sramans holy,
Men who toil in life,
Faithful fathers, loving children,
Husband and the wife,—
These to pain and separation,
Slavery and death,
I have doomed, and swept Kalinga
With destruction's breath !

3

" Let me seek for other trophies,
Win the spoils of faith,—
Peace and plenty, not disaster,
Life and love, not death !
Speak then to my farthest frontiers,
To each distant soil,
Warfare ends, the work of mercy
Henceforth is my toil !

4

" Syria's monarch Antiochus,
Egypt's Ptolemy,
Macedonian Antigonas,
Cyrenean Magas free,
Alexander of Epiros,—
These five kings of West
Have received my loving message,
Gospel true and blest !

5

Religious mission to Indian races

"Cholas and the mighty Pandyas,
Tamba-pannis meek,
Henaraja-Vismavasis,
And the Bactrian Greek,
Nabhakas and Nabha-pantis,
Bhojas inly stirred,
Andhras and the brave Pulindas
Have my tidings heard!

6

"Messengers of Piyadasi
To these lands are sent,
Grateful kings and listening nations
To his faith have bent;
Thus I win a brighter conquest
And a holier fame,
And a more than earthly gladness
Thrills my mortal frame!

7

"Rich and rare the golden fruitage
Of a life of faith,
Full and ample is the harvest
Gathered after death;
Hence the monarch Piyadasi
Carves this sacred line,
That his royal sons and grandsons
May to faith incline!

8

Let monarchs conquer by faith

" That the kings of earth hereafter
May all conquests shun,
Wrought by rapine and by bloodshed,
Deeds of darkness done;
That the monarchs may hereafter
Conquer realms by faith,
Fame on earth awaits such conquest,
Glory after death! "

Rock Edict, XIII.

VI

MUKTALATA, PRINCESS OF CEYLON

I

LIKE the bright moon's golden crescent,
Rising from the milky sea,
She was born with heavenly beauty
In Simhala bright and free.

2

On her birth a shower of bright pearls
From the skies auspicious came,
Hence they called her Muktalata,
Wreath of pearls,—the maiden's name!

3

How the Princess grew to womanhood

And she grew in grace and beauty,
Lanka's royal house to bless,
And as worth brings sweet contentment,
So her years brought loveliness.

4

Merchants from the famed Sravasti,
Happily it so befell,
Crossed the sea, to fair Simhala
Came their merchandise to sell.

5

And they sung the sacred *Gatha*,
As their nightly sleep they sought,
Sung the holy lay which teaches
Precepts that our Master taught.

6

From her inner palace chambers
Mukta heard the chanted lay,
Asked the merchants to her presence,
And its import bade them say.

7

And they told the raptured maiden,
"Princess! 'tis the Buddha's word,
He is bounteous to all creatures,
Of all creatures he is Lord!"

How the Princess heard of Buddha

8

And the pious-hearted princess
Heard the holy Buddha's name,
And a brightness flushed her forehead,
And a tremor shook her frame!

9

Eagerly the pea-fowl listens
To the cloud, presaging rain,
Eagerly the princess listened,—
Who this Lord?—she asked again.

10

To the princess, pious-hearted,
By her questions gratified,
Spake the merchants of the Buddha,
Lord of all creation wide.

11

Till awoke within her bosom
Memories of her previous birth,
And to them she gave a letter
For the Buddha, Lord of earth.

12

And the traders crossed the ocean,
Reached their own, their native land,
Gave the message to the Buddha,
Placed the letter in his hand.

13

How Buddha read the Princess's epistle

And our Master, all fore-knowing,—
Knowing all the princess wrote,—
Moved by tenderness and mercy,
Thus perused the maiden's note:

14

" Thy remembrance brings salvation,
Cures all passions, hate and strife,
And imparting righteous knowledge
Is like nectar to my life!"

15

Thus our saintly Lord and Master
Briefly read the pious scroll,
And a gentle smile betokened
All the workings of his soul.

16

And with skill and knowledge wondrous,
Which the painters never knew,
For the princess of Simhala
On a sheet his likeness drew.

17

By his mandate all the merchants
With their cargo sailed anew,
Reached Simhala, to the princess
Gave the sheet our Master drew.

How Buddha replied to the epistle

18

And the people viewed the painting
Placed upon a golden shelf,
And with honour contemplating
Seemed to see the Lord himself!

19

Written under that sweet likeness,
All the people, wondering truly,
Saw the holy Three Asylums,
Saw the Five Instructions holy;

20

And the Noble Eightfold Pathway
Deftly writ, with wisdom rife,
With the Doctrine of Causation,—
Life to death, and death to life!

21

Blazing bright in golden letters,
On it shone the Holy Word,—
Truth explained in beauteous language,
Written by our blessed Lord.

22

"Sufferers from sin and sorrow,
Leave this darksome vale of tears,
Serpent-fanged are worldly passions,
Trust in Him who quells all fears."

23

How the Princess was freed from worldly longings

And the monarch's noble daughter
Viewed the likeness fair and holy,
And was freed from worldly longings
Bred of ignorance and folly.

24

Tall and fair his golden likeness,
Broad his shoulders, mighty arms,
Eyelids closed in contemplation,
Stately nose and manly charms;

25

Beaming in his native beauty,
Ears and locks by art unaided,
Clad in russet,—like a mountain
By the evening's red cloud shaded;

26

Teaching duty by his bearing,
By his bright face teaching good,
Mercy by his soft eyes teaching,—
Such the form the princess viewed!

27

Bowing, till the budding blossoms
From her ears and ringlets rained,
With them earthly joys discarding,
Truth supreme the princess gained.

How the Princess found peace

28

In a moment's time achieving
Truth divine and Knowledge rare,
Lost in joy and pious wonder
Thus in gladness spake the fair:

29

"Chaser of the world's illusions,
Saintly Buddha, dwelling far,
Present by this radiant likeness,
Lovelier than the lotus-star;

30

"I have crossed the world's illusions,
Heart's true concentration found,
Pains and passions all have left me,—
Peace, like nectar, flows around!"

31

Thus she spake, and to the Buddha
Pearls and costly jewels sent,—
For the use of holy *Sangha*
With these gifts the merchants went;

32

O'er the sea, unto our Master,
In their ships the merchants came,—
Bowing unto him they rendered
Pearl and stone and costly gem.

How Buddha explained the doctrine of re-births

33

And our Master kindly listened
To the tale the merchants told,—
Questioned by the monk Ananda
Thus did Mukta's life unfold :

34

"Rohika, a servant woman,
In a Sakya's house who stayed,
Hath been born as Muktalata,
By her worth a princess made!

35

"Mahadhana, princely merchant,
In Benares lived of yore,
And his wife, a virtuous woman,
Ratnavati name she bore;

36

"And when died this Mahadhana,
Ratnavati, childless fair,
On a lofty holy *stupa*
Placed a necklace rich and rare;

37

"For this action, elevated,
She as Muktalata shone,
Born as Lanka's beauteous princess
Royal station she has won;

and the doctrine of Karma. Deeds yield their fruits

38

" Not at once, for pride of treasures
Stained her soul as merchant's wife,
Born as servant, cleansed of passion,
Next she lives her queenly life!

39

" Deeds that are by mortals rendered,
Good or bad upon this earth,
Yield their fruits in equal measure,
Ripened in a future birth!

40

" Holy life, a fragrant creeper,
Rooted well in righteous worth,
Bears its blossoms in this wide world,
Bears its fruit in after birth;

41

" Evil life, a poisonous creeper,
Rooted in unrighteous deed,
Yields on earth its vain delusions,
And hereafter cruel meed!

42

" In this lifetime ever fleeting,
Shun, ye men, all deeds unholy,
Bitter are the woes that follow,
Penitence pursueth folly;

43

The fruitage of virtue is nourished by the dew of mercy

"In the acts of grace rejoicing
Strive in faith and righteousness,
Nourished by the dew of Mercy
Virtue's fruitage comes to bless!"

From Kshemendra's Kalpalata, VII.

IV

THE BRIDAL OF UMA, BY KALIDASA

Date, circa 500 A.D.

The three centuries (500 to 800 A.D.) commencing with the time of Vikramaditya the Great may be called the Augustan era of later Sanscrit literature, and nearly all the great works which are popular in India to this day belong to this period.

Kalidasa, the greatest poet of this age, is best known to European readers by his immortal drama, Sakuntala. His narrative and descriptive poems are also popular in India; and among them, his Kumara-Sambhava is perhaps the best. Books, I, III, and V of this poem, virtually containing the entire story, have been translated in the following pages.

I

UMA'S BIRTH

The poem begins with a description of the Himalaya Mountains. The birth of Uma, her youth and beauty, and her first meeting with Siva, are then narrated in this Book.

I

The Himalaya mountains

HIMALAYA mountain-monarch,
Guarding regions of the north,
Stretching east to western ocean,
Seems to span the spacious earth.
As the cow gives milk to young ones,
So the earth to Himalay
Yielded wealth of wood and forest,
Gem and stone of purest ray.
And so bright the store of treasure,
Ice bedims it not, nor snow,
As the stain on moon's bright crescent
Darkens not its silver glow!
Rocks that glow like ruddy evening,
Tints that with the soft clouds blend,
Tempt the nymphs to paint their glances,
Teach them keener darts to send.
Peaks that rise above the rain cloud,
And in constant sunshine glow,

Ice-fields and mountain woods

Tempt the anchorite and hermit
From the mist and storm below.
Ice field, where in vain the hunter
Seeks for bloodstains washed by snow,
Strewn by pearls from slaughtered tuskers,
Teach him secret haunts to know.
And the barks on which in crimson
Whispered thoughts of love are written,
Serve as missives for the wood-nymphs,
Oft, alas, in secret smitten!

II

Woodland minstrels lift their voices
Rich in notes of woodland love,
Mountain breezes lend their music
Piping through the bamboo grove.
Stately Sal-trees broke by tuskers
Yield their gum so rich and rare,
Lend their fragrance to the greenwood,
Scenting sweet the mounting air.
Creepers, luminous in darkness,
In the lover's grottos gleam,
And like night-lamps self-illumined
Shed a soft and kindly beam.
And deep-bosomed forest damsels,
Moving with a languid grace,
Though they step o'er frozen ice-fields,
Oft frequent the trysting place!
Shadows fleeing from the sunlight
Shelter in the mountain's cave,
As the timid and the helpless
Seek for refuge with the brave.

Chowries wave their fans of silver
Gleaming like the moonbeams bright,
As to crownéd king his menials
Wave the Chamar silver-white.
And the mists that shade the grottos,
Deepening as they onward ride,
Often screen from ardent lovers
Charms the blushing nymph would hide!
Saturate with Ganga's moisture
Breezes cool the rocky soil,
Murmur through the mountain forest,
Cheer the hunter in his toil.
Lotus beds whence star-bright Rishis
Gather buds for holy rite,
Are by southern sun awakened
With a faint and crimson light.
And to dominate this wide earth,
And to prosper pious rites,
Himalay was made the loftiest
Of all lofty mountain heights!

Chowries whose tails make fans used in India

III

Lo! the mountain-monarch,
To his duty true,
Wedded sweet-eyed Mena,—
Saints her virtues knew;
Sported in love's dalliance
Nymph and monarch brave,
And the happy Mena
Gladsome promise gave!
Daksha's duteous daughter,—
Siva's former wife,—

Siva's first wife died and was born again as Uma, to be wedded to Siva again

Came as Mena's daughter,
    Took a newer life ;
Her as monarch's infant
    Queenly Mena bore,
As to wisdom wedded
    Virtue brings forth lore !
Flowers from heavens descended,
    Music cheered the morn,
Air was filled with gladness,
    When the babe was born ;
And with brighter beauty
    Queenly Mena shone,
Like the famed Vidura
    With her gem and stone !

IV

As the waxing moon in splendour
    Wears a bright and brighter ray,
So the sweet child sweetly added
    Lines of beauty day by day.
Parvati,—so gossips named her,
    Mountain-child of peerless fame,
Uma,—so her mother called her,
    Uma was her cherished name.
And on her the fondling father
    Eyes of soft affection bent,
As the bee is drawn at spring time
    By the blossoming mango's scent !
For as flame is to the bright lamp,
    Milky way to starry heaven,
Poetry to soul of genius,
    She unto her sire was given !

And the sands of Mandakini
Witnessed gentle Uma's play,
Girt by maidens of the mountain,
Merry as the morning's ray.
And as swans of Ganga's waters,
Light to lustrous plants of earth,
Grace and culture came to Uma,—
Culture of a former birth!

Uma passed her childhood where the Ganges issues out of the Himalayas

V

Youth disclosed a woman's beauty,
Nature's graces void of art,
Wine's sweet langour void of madness,
Love's soft glamour not his dart.
And as painter's pencil traces
Blushing bloom of brow and face,
Or as sunbeams ope the lotus,
Youth disclosed the maiden's grace!
From her feet bright tints of crimson
Seemed to drop at ever pace,
Lotus waved by gentle zephyrs
Move not with a softer grace.
And her anklets sweetly tinkled
As the princess walked in state,
Stately white birds caught the music,
Uma caught their graceful gait!
Tapering limbs in beauty fashioned
Shewed the Maker's highest skill,
When He shaped all forms in nature,
Uma's form was loveliest still.
For all bright and beauteous objects,
Lithesome shape or slender tree,

Uma attains her youth

Were but models rudely fashioned,—
In her blent harmoniously!
Softly swelling, sweetly rounded,
Uma shewed her girdled charms,—
More than mortal woman's beauty,
Destined for immortal arms;
And a dark gem decked the girdle
Cast its radiance clear and keen,—
Shaded lines with pencilled beauty
Marked her gently swelling skin.
Curve and dimple sweetly moulded,
On her lithe form softly traced,
Were like steps young Love had fashioned
Nestling in her heaving breast;
And her young and swelling bosom
Rose voluptuous; scarce I ween,
Tenderest fibre of the lotus
Found a resting place between!

VI

Soft the blossoms of Sirisa,
Softer Uma's rounded arms,—
Were they chains young Love had fashioned
For the God who owned her charms?
On her neck and heaving bosom
Hung the pearls in graceful cluster,
Did they lend her brighter beauty,
Did her bosom lend them lustre?
If the lotus oped its petals
In the beauty of the night,
Moon-lit blossoms then might rival
Uma's face serene and bright!

If the jasmine bloomed on coral,
Pearls on rosy leaf were set,
Uma's red lips, teeth of whiteness,
Nature then might imitate!
And when from those red lips issued
Voice of music sweet and clear,
In the woods that startled Kokil
Hushed his lay that voice to hear!
And her glances! Did the wild deer
Learn the dark charm of her eye,—
Did she from the deer of forest
Learn that secret mystery?
Archéd eye-brows darkly shaded
Thrilled the gazer's beating heart,
Were they young Love's bow of prowess
Quick to send the fatal dart?
And in dark and clustering ringlets
Fell her ample wealth of hair,
Did the long haired mountain Chowrie
Hide in shame within her lair?
Fairest forms and shapes in nature
Richest tint and softest shade,
Were in harmony united
To create this mountain maid!

Her surpassing loveliness

VII

Heavenly minstrel Narad,
Saw her beauty's pride,—
Saw, the girl was destined
To be Siva's bride.
And no other bridegroom
Sought her royal sire,—

Siva passes his days in prayer and contemplation in the Himalaya mountains

Sacred gift is offered
 Only to the Fire.
Nor to high-souled Siva
 Was an offer laid,—
He must seek and conquer
 Who would win a maid.
Since his former consort
 Left her mortal life,
Siva was a wanderer,
 Sought no second wife.
And where Ganga's waters
 Washed the mountain wood,
In the fragrant forests
 He in penance stood.
There, his rustic menials,
 Decked in leaf and flower,
Sported on the red rock
 Rested in the bower.
There, the bull of Siva
 On the ice-field stood,
Viewed by beasts with terror,
 Monarch of the wood.
There the homeless Siva
 Prayed alone and dwelt,
Who shall tell what purpose
 In his heart he felt?
And the mountain-monarch
 Held him as his guest,
Bade his duteous daughter
 Wait upon his hest.
And on Siva waited
 Uma meek of eye,
Woman's beauty moves not

Him whose thoughts are high.
And she culled the blossoms,
Lit the sacred fire,
Fetched the grass and water,
For Kailasa's Sire!

Banished Gods seek the help of the God of love

II

UMA'S YOUTH

Indra and his host of Gods had been expelled from heaven by the Titans. They had been told that a son of Siva, borne by Uma, could alone lead them back to victory and to heaven. They therefore sent Kandarpa the God of Love to the earth, to inspire Siva with an affection for the mountain maid.

I

BANISHED by the conquering Titans
Homeless lived the gods of heaven,—
Indra turned to Love for succour,
Wondrous power to Love is given!
Seated next to sovran Indra,
Greeted by his gracious word,
God of Love with due obeisance
Questioned thus his anxious lord:
"Speak thy mandate, Lord of creatures,
Thou canst probe their purpose best,
And thy summons is a favour,
Higher grace,—thy royal hest!
Who by penance long and arduous
Seeks to wrest thy heavenly throne?—

The God of love boasts of his power

Shaft of Love can conquer penance,
Anchorites may prowess own!
Who renouncing earthly pleasures
Seeks the life of loneliness?—
Woman's glance can vanquish hermits,
Monks their magic power confess!
Who, by Sukra taught in wisdom,
Longs to tread the narrow way?—
As the flood sweeps o'er a kingdom,
Love o'erwhelms poor wisdom's sway!
Hath some dame of rigid virtue
With a passion fired thy heart?—
She shall flame with answering passion,
Women know my conquering dart!
Hath some wronged, disdainful damsel
Turned on thee her wrathful eye?—
She shall pine with longing langour,
On a bed of leaves shall lie!
Rest thy bolt, grim God of thunder,
Wondrous is my softer dart,—
Pouting red lips humble heroes,
Bright eyes tame the Titan's heart!
Mighty Siva, God of bright gods,
Owns my shaft's resistless charms,—
Love and Springtime well may conquer
Trident-wielding Siva's arms!"

II

Rashly thus Kandarpa boasted
Power to quell Kailasa's Lord,
And, well-pleased, the God of thunder
Took him promptly at his word:

"True my friend! The forkéd lightning
Is my all resistless dart,
Yet on saints my bolt is powerless,
Saint and sinner own thy art!
Well I know thy might resistless,
Ask thee mighty work to share,
Who but world-sustaining Sesa
Weight of solid earth could bear?
Thou hast said, on peerless Siva
Speeds thy unresisted dart,
Thou hast therein told the wishes
Bright gods cherish in their heart;
Born of Him, a conquering leader
Will o'er Titan foes prevail,
But to love and happy wedding
Who but thee can Siva quell?
May he eye with soft affection
Daughter of the mountain king,
She will make a worthy consort
And to gods their fortunes bring;
She, by mountain-monarch's mandate,
Waits on Siva in his rites;
So the heavenly nymphs have told me,
Those who scan the mountain heights;
Speed, then, in this heavenly mission
High success and fame attain,
For the task awaits thy effort
As the seed awaits the rain!
May thy shining dart, Kandarpa
Win us heaven's perennial bliss,
Fame awaits on all achievements,
Highest fame on deed like this;
Gods are suppliants for thy favour,

Indra urges him to try his power on Siva

A son of Siva born of Uma will lead the gods back to heaven

Weal of worlds awaits thy power,
Bloodless is thy high achievement,
Glory is thy destined dower!
God of Spring will work conjointly,
He is e'er thy helping friend,
When the red flame springs in radiance,
Winds their aid spontaneous lend!"
Indra spake; and gently smiling
Stroked the beaming God of Love,
Proud Kandarpa bowed obeisance,
Left for Himalaya's grove.

III

Where in contemplation
Siva lived alone,
Young Love flew with ardour
To his duty prone.
And the peace-disturber
Merry Spring-time came,
Rousing hearts of hermits
To unwonted flame.
Southern sun untimely
Turned his chariot north,
And the south wind's kisses
Waked to joy the earth!
Asok bloomed spontaneous,
Touched by maid nor wife,
Though 'tis said a woman
Wakes that tree to life!
Mango-flowers, leaf-feathered,
Where like darts of flame,
Bees like graven letters
Marked the Love-God's name!

All nature wakes to life in the spring-time

Scentless Karnikara
Maidens do not prize,—
Nature oft to beauty
Deeper worth denies.
Red Palasa blossomed
In its crimson drest,—
Love's caressing tokens
On the woodland's breast.
And the blushing green wood
Glowed like nymph of sky,—
Mango-shoots her red lips,
Bees her dark bright eye!

IV

Wild deer with new ardour
Ranged among the trees,
By the flower-dust blinded
Sought the southern breeze.
Kokils fed on mangoes
Chanted sweet and clear,
Nymphs forgot their coyness
That wild lay to hear!
And with ruddier beauty
Kim-purushas shone,
Lips of deeper crimson,
Bosoms warmed by sun!
Aye, the pale-faced hermits
Felt an inward strife,
From their silent penance
Woke to surging life.
And all forest creatures
Felt the wondrous power,

All living creatures feel the impulses of love

And in love's sweet dalliance
    Spent the glowing hour!
Bee pursued the female,
    Drank from flower she tasted,
Black buck closed his eyelids,
    By his partner rested;
Tusker drank the water
    Which the female gave,
With his mate the Chukwa
    Sported on the wave!
On the lips of wood-nymphs,
    Faint with toil of song,
Flushed with wine and langour,
    Swains impassioned hung;
And with lips of red-leaf,
    And their flower-gemmed breast,
Creepers round the tall trees
    In love's dalliance prest!

V

Vainly rose the voice of music,
    Vain the breezes breathed of love,
Deep in holy contemplation
    Siva sat within his grove.
And outside the hut of creepers
    Watchful Nandi held his wand,
Placed upon his lips the finger,
    Held in silence all the land!
Bird and bee were hushed and voiceless,
    Red deer ranged not in that wood,
By his mandate all the confines
    Like a painted landscape stood.

Sublime description of Siva rapt in contemplation

Quelled by Siva's lofty presence,
Even the God of Love withdrew,
In a bush of wild Nameru
Half concealed him from his view!
On a seat of Deva-daru,
Covered by the tiger's skin,
Silent-seated, still and stately,
Siva's ample form was seen;
Frame erect in contemplation,
Shoulders builded deep and broad,
Lotus palms conjoined in worship,
Moveless sat the mighty God!
Serpents twined around his tresses,
Beads depended from his ear,
From his blue throat, deeper-shaded,
Hung the dark skin of the deer;
And beneath the ample eye-brows
Half was seen each radiant eye,
Shaded by the moveless lashes
Fixed in contemplation high;
Like the deep cloud,—dark but silent,
Like the ocean,—vast but still,
Like the flame,—by winds unshaken,
Dreaded God of dauntless will!
And a radiance bright and beaming,
Which his ample forehead flung
Lighted up the lunar crescent
On his God-like locks that hung;
Quelled each outer sense aud feeling.
Fixed each sense in lofty thought,
He whom sages call ETERNAL
In his self the Great Self sought!

Advent of Uma on the scene

VI

Him,—inviolate and unconquered,—
God of Love with awe surveyed,
From his trembling, nerveless fingers
Bow and arrow fell in dread;
But his faint heart filled with gladness,
Flame of courage leapt to light,
As, encircled by her maidens,
Beauteous Uma burst on sight!
Bearing wreaths of Karni-kara,
Red Asoka's ruby store,
Garlanded with Sindhu-vara,
Wealth of spring the maiden bore;
Wearing scarf like molten sunlight
On her swelling bosom laid,
Like a blossom-weighted creeper
Softly stepped the mountain-maid!
Holding oft the flowery girdle
Slipping from her narrow zone,—
Brighter bow-string for his arrows
God of Love did never own;—
Waving back with fan of lotus
Timidly the thirsty bee,—
Well her lips might tempt the insect
From the honey of the tree;—
Fresh and fragrant from the forest
Bright and beauteous Uma came,
And a new born hope and ardour
Thrilled Kandarpa's heart to flame!
Softly in the grove she entered,
As the God immersed in thought
Found within his radiant bosom

Holy Light which he had sought;
Slowly then from contemplation
Lord of creatures, Siva woke,
Wore a lighter grace and station
When the holy trance was broke.

Siva wakes from his contemplation

VII

Watchful Nandi spake of Uma,
Waiting with her duteous love,
Gracious Siva gave permission,
And she came within the grove.
And her maidens bowed to Siva,
Strewed around his blessed feet
Flower and young leaf they had gathered,
Fresh and fragrant, soft and sweet.
Uma too, in pious reverence,
Bent to do obeisance meet,
And the buds that starred her tresses
Sweetly rained on Siva's feet!
"Live to be a dear-loved consort,
Live to be a loving wife,—"
Thus the bright God blessed the maiden,
For the gods can bless our life.
And as moth unto the bright flame,
God of Love flew to the scene,
Watching this auspicious moment
With his arrow bright and keen!
Garland of the seed of lotus,
Ripened by Mandakni's wave,
Wreathed by her own rosy fingers,
Uma unto Siva gave.
Gently touching hands so tender
Siva took the offered wreath,

Love's mischievous interference and summary punishment

God of Love then took his arrow
    Keener than the shaft of death!
Silent heaved the heart of Siva
    Like the ocean's heaving swell,—
On her face and lips of coral
    His impassioned glances fell.
She with woman's inborn instinct
    Knew the import of the glance,—
Brow and bosom flushed and crimsoned,
    Uma stood as in a trance!
Then with strong and godlike effort
    Siva quelled the rising flame,
Sought with cold and cruel glances
    Whence the sudden impulse came;
And he marked the young Kandarpa,
    Leaning still on bended knee,
Bow of blossoms still encircled,
    Right hand drawn unto his eye!
Then arose a mighty anger,—
    Bright Gods know his wrath too well,
As from cloud the lurid flashes,
    From his eye the red flame fell;
"Spare, O spare!" the bright Gods uttered,—
    Ere these accents, winged their way,
Burnt by Siva's flashing glances
    Lifeless Love in ashes lay!

VIII

With the young Kandarpa,
    Gentle Rati fell,
Grief hath power o'er bright Gods,
    Sorrows, who can quell?

As on tree the lightning
On them fell his wrath,
He to unknown regions
Silent sought his path!
Silent wended Uma
To her home again,—
Speaks no maid her sorrows
When she loves,—in vain!
But her father fathomed
Feelings unexprest,
Saw the tears she shed not,
Held her in his breast!

Siva leaves the mountains. Uma retires in sadness

III

UMA'S PENANCE AND LOVE

1

For she loved and lost,—sweet Uma
Did herself no longer prize,—
What is woman's winning beauty
If it please not lover's eyes?
She would move by lofty penance
If her graces failed to move,—
Win by worth and not by beauty
Life's fruition,—heart's true love!
Vainly strove the doting mother
To restrain the wayward child,
Held her in her loving bosom,
Spake to her in accents mild:
"Stay at home, for arduous penance
Suits not, child, thy tender make,

Uma resolves on a severe penance

Light-winged bees may rest on blossoms,
Birds their silken frame would break!"
Still with mother's love she pleaded,
Vainly urged a mother's force,
Woman's will and running river,
Who can turn them from their course?
By her maids did silent Uma
To her sire her purpose own,—
She would be a lonely hermit,
She would dwell in forests lone;
He had read her secret purpose,
He approved her dauntless will,—
Uma in her youth and beauty
Went to Gauri's lonely hill!

II

Pearls, that in a graceful cluster
On her neck and shoulders fell,
She forsook; and barks of wild trees
Scarce enclosed her bosom's swell;
And her rich and raven tresses
Wildly matted now she wore,
So on wild moss blows the lotus
Where no bee purloins its store!
Holy strings of grass of Munja
Did her girdle chain replace,
Dyed her skin with deeper crimson
By its rustic rude embrace.
Brow and bosom, lip and eyelash
Knew no more the toilet's need,
For her soft and reddened fingers
Culled the grass and told the bead.

Retires to a hill forest and discards all comforts of life

Flowers that dropped from scented tresses
Strewed no more a royal bed,
On the bare rocks Uma rested
Pillowed on her arms her head!
To the creeper, zephyr-shaken,
Yielded she her movements light,
To the antelope of forest
Lent her glances soft and bright;
To the plants with mother's tendance
Drink of water did she pour,
Like a first born dear to Uma,
Dear as child she later bore;
To the trusting deer of forest
Gave she grain for which they came,
Loved their eyes so soft and tender
Till her maidens blushed with shame!
Baths performed, the fires she lighted,
Hymns she sang of holy love,
Till the sages came to see her,
Holiest hermit in the grove;
Beasts forgot their mutual struggle,
Trees with gifts of blossoms stood,
Bright fires blazed upon the altar,
Holy was her hermit-wood!

III

Sterner rites and penance
Now the maid begun,
For by highest effort
Highest meed is won!
And her frame so tender
Hermit's toil did bear,

Her severe penance in summer, in the rains, and in winter

Like a golden lotus
    Strong, though fresh and fair!
Flaming fires in summer
    Round her radiant shone,
As she sat in prayer
    Gazing on the sun;
Like a sun-browned lotus,
    Crimsoned was her face,
And a darker shadow
    Dimmed her eye's soft grace;
Springs that fed the creeper
    Drink to Uma brought,
Save the moon's sweet moisture,
    Food she never sought!
Rains that after summer
    Cooled the parchéd soil,
Drew a sigh of gladness
    From her in her toil;
On her eye and red lip,
    On her bosom's swell,
Rolled the fresh born rain drop,
    Glistening as it fell;
And the midnight witnessed,
    With its lightning eye,
Her in rain and tempest
    'Neath the open sky!
After rains the winter
    Saw the tireless maid
In the ice-bound water
    Where the Chukwas played;
And her lips were parted,
    Fragrant was her face,
Like a water lotus

A hermit youth comes to her holy wood

Soft and sweet her grace !
Fruit and shoot spontaneous
Are the hermit's due,
She no wild fruit tasted,
She no young shoot knew ;
Thus by long endurance,
Tender though her frame,
She than holiest hermits
Won a holier fame !

IV

Beaming with a righteous radiance,
Came a youth when spring time came,
Wearing skins and matted tresses,
Glassing Heaven in human fame !
Honour to the lofty stranger
And obeisance Uma paid,
Even on her, a forest dweller,
Grace of form its impress made ;
She unto the pious pilgrim
Fruit and crystal water brought,
He unto fair Mena's daughter
Courteously disclosed his thought.
"Doth this wood provide, fair maiden,
Grass and fuel for thy rite,
Water for thy day's ablutions,
For thy worship blossoms bright ?
Doth the creeper of the woodland,
Nourished by thy tender care,
Ceaseless bloom in leaf and blossom
Like thy pale lips soft and fair ?
And the red deer of the forest,
Fed by thee both morn and late,

Enquires about her penance

Do they claim thy sweet affection
As thy glance they imitate?
Grace of form hides inner beauty,
Truly thus our sages say,
For thy deeds to holy hermits
Well may point the righteous way.
Not this sky-descended Ganga,
Wafting flowers from heavenly hands,
Like thy spotless fame and virtue
Sanctifies these sacred lands!
Holy rites than worldly objects
Sure a higher charm must claim,
Since despising rank and riches
Thou dost long for hermit's fame.
Deem me, fair one, not a stranger,
Since thou holdst me as thy guest,
On brief words in candour spoken
Love and friendship often rest;
Pardon, then, a friend's presumption,
If as friend I dare to speak,
Brahmans are by nature curious,
And for further light I seek.

V

"Thou art born of highest lineage,
Decked with charms few women know,—
Wherefore then this arduous penance,
What more gifts can Heaven bestow?
Women stung with shame and insult
Oft in forest shades reside,—
Can such sorrow touch thee maiden
In thy youth and beauty's pride?

Also about her secret motive

Who could in thy father's mansions,
    Princess, cause thy heart to bleed,
Who could from the jewelled serpent
    Wrest the jewel in his greed?
Wherefore hidest in these wild barks
    Bloom of youth and beauty's might,
Doth the young night, star-resplendent,
    Wear the morning's garish light?
Not for joys of heaven thy penance,
    For this realm is bright as sky,
And for loved and worthy suitor,
    Need a beauteous maiden sigh?
Yet that sigh, that heaving bosom,
    Speaks a woman's secret smart,
Who could be thy loved and chosen,
    Chosen, who could loveless part?
Can he mark unmoved thy penance,
    Forehead which no flowers adorn,
Bloodless brow and matted tresses
    Dust-embrowed like ripened corn?
Can he coldly view thy bosom,
    Lighted erst by gem and stone,
Shaded now by summer's radiance,
    Lightless like the morning moon?
Drunk with fortune's fickle favour,
    Darkly lives he in a trance,
Who with eager love and passion
    Meets not Uma's loving glance!
Speak thy secret! If thy feelings
    To some errant youth incline,
I have somewhat earned by penance,
    Half of what I own be thine!"

Uma's maiden recounts to the hermit the sad tale of Uma's love

VI

Uma silent listened,
    Spake not in reply,
To her waiting maiden
    Turned her bashful eye;
She by Uma's mandate
    Mournful tale revealed,
Why she toiled in penance,
    Why her love concealed?
"She the gods despising
    Fixed on Him her thought,
Who hath conquered passion,—
    Beauty moves him not!
Young Love's cruel arrow,
    Useless on the God,
Fell on Uma's bosom,—
    Drank her dearest blood!
In her father's mansions
    Then she found no rest,
In the icy grottos
    Ceaseless burnt her breast;
In the midnight silence
    She of Siva sung,
Nymphs of wood and mountain
    Wept to hear her song!
Pale light of the morning
    Saw her in a dream,
Clasping empty shadow,
    Calling Siva's name;
Red light of the gloaming
    Saw his face pourtrayed,
To the painted image
    She her thoughts conveyed!

And the story of Uma's long penance

Till at last despairing,
Left her father's home,
To engage in penance
And in woods to roam.
On the trees she planted
Red ripe fruit hath grown,
But her love's young sapling
Joy nor hope hath known.
Will the cruel Siva
Ever quench her sorrow,
As the rain of summer
Fills the thirsty furrow?"
Uma still was silent,
Still enquired the youth,
If this was a fable,
If this was the truth;
Counting beads of crystal,
Bending down her head,
Bashful, tearful Uma
In a whisper said:
"Thou hast heard all truly
What this heart hath moved,
If I hoped too wildly,
Greatly I have loved!"

VII

"Known to me,"—the hermit answered—
"He, the object of thy love,
And forgive me, gentle maiden,
If thy choice, I scarce approve!
Scarce I fathom, lovely Uma,
How these gentle hands of thine

H

The hermit speaks slightingly of Siva

Shall, with wedding wreath encircled,
Clasp his hands which snakes entwine ;
And a young wife's bridal garment,
Traced with birds of plumage fair,
Scarce will match his blood-stained mantle,
Skins and barks he loves to wear !
In thy father's stately mansions
Flowery paths thy feet have trod,—
Wilt thou now on sites unholy
Wander with a homeless God?
Fragrant with the scent of *Chandan*
Is thy young and virgin breast,—
On his bosom and smeared with ashes
Wilt thou Uma, take thy rest?
Royal tuskers decked with trappings
Well beseem a royal bride,—
Wilt thou learn, my gentle princess,
Siva's graceless bull to ride?
Lightless is the lunar crescent
Which depends from Siva's head,—
Loveless too shall be the consort
Whom the uncouth God shall wed!
Wild his mein, obscure his lineage,
Wealth nor rank his guise betrays,
Grace he owns nor courtly virtue,
By which bridegrooms win our praise!
Turn, O turn from such a suitor,
Nor to him thy beauty yield,
Not on darksome funeral places
Holy men their altars build!"

VIII

Uma replies to him in anger

Quivering lip and archéd eyebrow,
And her bosom's angry swell,
Spake of Uma's rising passion
As on him her glances fell!
"Knowing little, speakest lightly,"—
Proudly thus the maid replied,—
"Lofty souls of unknown splendour
Flippant mortals thus deride!
Refuge of the wide creation,
Ruler of Immortals' fate,
Doth he brook our mortal customs,
Pomp and pageantry and state?
Void of wealth,—but source of riches,
Homeless,—ranging earth and sky,
Wild of mein,—his grace pervadeth,
Who can comprehend the High?
Wearing gems or coiling serpents,
Broidered lace or skin and skull,
Who can guess his real image,
Glassed in worlds, pervading all?
And if ashes smear his bosom,
They can bless and sanctify
Men below and bright Immortals,
Dwellers of the azure sky!
And if sacred bull his emblem,
Indra with obeisance meet
From his crown of heavenly blossoms
Drops the flower-dust on its feet!
Didst thou say,—obscure his lineage
And unknown his race on earth?—

Uma finds her loved and lost

Bright Gods own him as Creator,
First Creator hath no birth!
But thou speakest as thou knowest,
Cease thy wrangling and depart,
Be his virtues great or scanty,
He hath won my faithful heart!
Open not thy lips unholy,
Tell me not that tale of shame,
Not alone the man who slanders,
He who listens shares the blame!"

IX

Turned away the damsel
From the stranger guest,—
Through the bursting wild bark
Heaved her angry breast!
Smiling he embraced her,
All disguise removed,—
Uma gazed in wonder,
'Twas her lost and loved!
Like a trembling lotus
Shook her tender frame,
O'er her brow and bosom
Quick the red blood came!
Still with foot uplifted,
Stayed not, could not go,
Like a rock bound torrent,
Stopped its onward flow!
"Maiden," so spake Siva,
"Take this hand of mine,
Won by love and penance
Henceforth I am thine!"

With a holier beauty
        Heavenly Uma shone,
For by toil and duty
        Destiny is won!

For Destiny is won by righteous toil

V

THE PENANCE OF ARJUN, BY BHARAVI

Date, circa 600 A.D.

THE poet Bharavi lived shortly after Kalidasa. His great poem *Kiratarjumyam* describes in eighteen Books how Arjun won celestial arms by his penance and valour. Books I, III, VI, XI and XII of the original poem tell the main story, and have been translated in the following pages. Some verses from Book XVIII of the original have been added at the end.

BOOK I

DRAUPADI'S REMONSTRANCE

King Yudhishthir had lost his kingdom, and had retired into forests with his wife and brothers. He sent a forester to observe how his foe ruled the kingdom. The forester returned, and gave a glowing account of Duryodhan's administration. Yudhishthir's wife listened to this account with a woman's jealousy, and counselled instant war to recover the lost kingdom.

I

The messenger returns to the banished king with tidings

Sent to Kuru-land to fathom
How Duryodhan ruled his men,
He,—a dweller of the forest,—
Came once more to Dwaita's glen.
Freely to the King Yudhishthir,
He, Duryodhan's glories told,
For they love not fulsome lying,
Those who serve the true and bold.
Strong of heart, the exiled monarch
Urged the spy his tale to tell,
Rich in language, deep in import,
Clear the words that from him fell!

He narrates his tale

II

" Who by King of men is trusted
Loves not to deceive his lord,
Pardon, then, if free my accents,—
Seldom true is honeyed word !
False the friend who basely flatters,
False the king who brooks a lie,
Only those who join in virtue
Conquer Fortune's favours high.
I, a dweller of the woodlands,
Deep designs but dimly trace,
If I comprehend thy foeman,
'Tis, O monarch, by thy grace!
Seated on the throne of nations,
Still he dreads thee, exiled lord,
Realm, by trick of dice he conquered,
Rules by righteous deed and word;
And with seeming virtue vested
Still he apes thy inborn grace,—
Better war with open foeman
Than communion with the base!
Veiling well his pride and passion
Manu's path he seeks to tread,
Toiling noon and dewy evening
Kuru's glories strives to spread.
And he treats as friends his menials,
Treats his friends as nearest kin,
While a semblance of affection
Darkly hides his thoughts within!
Still with equal love the monarch
Courts each kingly virtue well,—
Varying graces sought and conquered

In his heart harmonious dwell!
Bounty speaks his royal kindness,
Gifts with royal favours flow,
And his presents, never ceasing,
Only men of virtue know.
Nor for profit, nor in anger,
But to guard the righteous cause,
On his foe or on his children
Visits sins with equal laws.
Trusty are his palace soldiers,
Dauntless are his brow and face,
Bounteous are his sacrifices,
Endless is his royal grace.
And his plans devised by wisdom,
And pursued with silent toil,
Spread for him a happy future,
Bless the children of the soil!

And speaks of the reigning king's glory

III

"Cars and steeds of warrior-chieftains
Throng his palace halls around,
Tuskers sent by friendly monarchs
With their perfume fill the ground.
Kuru-lands are rich in harvests,
Ripening without tillers' toil,
Ask no rain, since Kuru's monarch
Showers his blessings on the soil.
And his rule of peace and plenty
Blesses towns and fertile fields,
And impregnate with his bounty
Earth her ample produce yields!
Chieftains from each town and castle,
Warriors famed in toil and strife,

The messenger concludes his story

Muster, not against their monarch,
But to guard him with their life.
And his spies can darkly fathom
Deep device of rival kings,
His device,—like work of Nature,—
Is revealed by fruit it brings!
Never bends his bow in battle,
Frowns his forehead never shade,
For his rule his subjects cherish
Like a garland on their head.
Aye, upon his gallant younger
He hath placed his regal might,
Saint-like, from the world retiring,
He performs each holy rite!
Conqueror of all his foemen,
Lord of earth begirt by sea,
Master of a rule unbounded,—
Still Duryodhan quakes at thee;
Let his courtiers name Yudhishthir,
Speak of Arjun's might of arm,
And the monarch bends his forehead
Like a snake subdued by charm!
Bent is he to do thee battle,
Be prepared thy foe to meet,—
This, O King, my humble message,
Such, I lay it at thy feet."

IV

Then the woodsman, honoured duly,
Went his way o'er hill and dale,
And Yudhishthir to his consort
Told once more the wond'rous tale.

Dark remembrance of her insults
    In her heaving bosom woke,
And, to rouse her husband's anger,
    Drupad's daughter proudly spoke.

The wife of the banished king advises instant war to recover the lost kingdom

V

"Counsel to a sapient monarch
    Is rebuke from woman weak,
But ignoring wifely duty,
    Pardon, if my feelings speak.
Mighty warriors, thy forefathers,
    Held their rule o'er Kuru's land,
But, as tuskers cast their garlands,
    Thou hast hurled it from thy hand!
Weak are they who with the wily
    Deal not with responsive wile,
For like darts on mail-less warriors
    Artful foemen on them steal.
Weak art thou who hast forsaken
    Glory of thy ancient house,—
More than life by warriors cherished,
    Dearer than their wedded spouse!

VI

"Godlike man! Now sadly treading
    Paths despised by proud and free,
Doth not rising wrath consume thee
    As the flames consume the tree?
Men spontaneous yield to heroes
    Who have will to face their foes,
But for faint, forgiving creatures
    Love nor friend nor foeman knows!

Laments the fall of her husband

Sandal-graced was royal Bhima,—
  Dust-besmeared he roams the hills,
Scarce I know, O soul of virtue,
  If thy heart with pity thrills.
Conqueror of northern nations,
  Arjun scattered wealth and gold,—
Mark him now, O saintly hermit,
  Bark-clad, sleeping on the wood.
And the twins, thy youngest brothers,
  Princes born and great and good,—
Mark them roaming in the jungle,
  Even like tuskers of the wood!
Scarce I guess thy feelings, monarch,
  Strange and diverse are our hearts,
But reflection on thy sorrow
  Cruel grief to me imparts.
Erst my lord from royal slumber
  Waked to hear the song of praise,
Now outstretched on jungle heather
  Hears the cry the jackals raise.
Erst on food by Brahmans tasted
  Lived my king of mighty name,
Now he feeds on forest berries
  Pale and lightless,—like his fame!
On thy feet, on jewels resting,
  Vassal kings their blossoms dropped,
Now they range the thorny woodlands
  By the deer or hermit cropped.
Most I grieve,—insulting foemen
  Mock thy low dejected state,—
Heroes win a higher glory
  If they strive with adverse fate!

VII

And urges him to recover his own

Conquer back thy glory,
Vengeful schemes devise,
Anchorites, not heroes,
Meek forbearance prize.
For if kings and chieftains
Bore their insults tame,
Lost were worth of warriors
Lost were monarch's fame!
Or if patient suffering
Still for thee hath charms,
Prate thy hymns like hermits,
Leave these kingly arms!
But a higher duty
Fits thy royal fame,
Break this plighted treaty,—
Treaty of our shame.
Monarchs bent on conquests
Fasten on their foe
Blame for breach of treaty,—
Blame for war and woe.
Pale from loss of glory,
Weak from loss of might,
Rise like sun in splendour,—
Quell this darksome night!

BOOK II

VYASA'S ADVICE

The remonstrance of Yudhishthir's wife was in vain. Yudhishthir had plighted his word, and would not depart from the treaty. At last the great saint Vyasa came on a visit to him, told him that war was inevitable, and advised him to send his brother Arjun to perform penances in order to win celestial arms.

Vyasa comes on a visit to the banished king

I

BEAMING with a gentle lustre
Soft as rays of autumn night,
Graced with auburn locks that clustered
Like a cloud of golden light,—
Glowing with a god-like mercy
In his more than human face,
Filling every living creature
With responsive love and grace,—
Speaking by his look and gesture
Peace that dwells in realms aloft,
Waking trust and true affection
By his glances sweet and soft,—
Herald of the holy Vedas
Vyasa to the monarch went,
And the courteous King Yudhishthir
Questioned thus the mighty Saint.

II

"Unattained by life-long merit
Is such favour great and high,

Vyasa's message to Yudhishthir

Like a holy life's fruition,
Like the rain from cloudless sky!
Holy rites have borne their harvest,
Brahmans' blessings brought their meed,
For thy sight is highest honour,
Truest blessing in my need!
Vedic Bard! Thy grace can conquer
Ills with which this earth is rife,
And thy love like love of BRAHMA
Sanctifies our mortal life!
Not the moon's benignant radiance
Cheers my sad and lightless eye,
But my heart forgets its sadness
Mighty Saint! since thou art nigh!
Thy desires I may not question,
Peaceful souls have no desires,
But a wish to hear thy utterance
My enquiring heart inspires."
Thus in graceful words the Monarch
To the Bard of Vedas prayed,
Anxious for the Monarch's glory
He unto Yudhishthir said.

III

"He who strives for earthly glory
Bears for all impartial love,
He who strives for peace and virtue
Should with higher justice move,
Yet my partial heart, Yudhishthir,
For thy virtues leans to thee,—
Virtue binds the lonesome hermit
From all earthly bondage free!

Vyasa foretells war

Are ye not of royal lineage
  Like the youth who fills the throne,
Hath his father lost his reason
  Thus to wrench from you your own?
And will Fortune help a warrior
  Who on Karna places trust,
Doth not faith with false and faithless
  Lead to fame and honour lost?
When they left the righteous pathway,
  You remained in virtue strong,
When they changed, still true and changeless
  You forgave the proud man's wrong.
And they sought to shame you vainly,
  Man of piety and love,
Every trial, wrong and insult
  Higher virtue in you prove.

IV

"Listen yet; by valour only
  You can win in battle's hour,
For your foe is strong in combat,
  Boundless in his wealth of power.
Jamadagni's son who conquered
  Thrice seven times the kings of earth,
Great though he,—he owns with terror
  Bhishma's greater, mightier worth;
Death is powerless, Death is conquered,
  By that chief's resistless might,
And the field of battle trembles
  When he enters on the fight!
Doughty Drona in the battle
  Speeds his darts in furious ire,

Like a world-consuming furnace
Shooting forth its tongues of fire
Archer Karna learnt his lessons
From great Jamadagni's son,
And the King of Terrors trembles
At his deeds of valour done!
These are chiefs, believe me Monarch,
Whom in battle thou shalt face,
Arm thyself by toil and penance,
Seek celestial help and grace;
Let young Arjun seek the weapons
Gods themselves by worship crave,—
This, Yudhishthir, is my message,
Win the gift that speeds the brave!"

Vyasa counsels preparation

V

Then the gallant archer Arjun
Stept forth reverent and slow,
Bending at his elder's mandate
Like a student bending low;
And the gift of saintly Vyasa,—
Mantra of the holy spell,—
As the sunlight falls on lotus,
On the valiant Arjun fell.
And the *mantra's* holy radiance,
Which the warrior proudly wore,
Oped his inner eye of reason,
Filled his heart with sacred lore;
And his form betokened glory,
And his heart was fixed and strong,
Vyasa spake of penance holy
To the warrior brave and young.

Arjun prepares to part

"Strengthened by this *mantra*, Arjun,
Yield thy warrior-pride to none,
Girt in arms perform thy penance,
Holy rites by hermits done;
And this Yaksha guide will lead thee
To the lofty golden hill,
There, perform thy sacred duty,
Do the Thunder-Wielder's will!"
Speaking thus unto the warrior
Vyasa vanished from his view,
And obedient to his mandate
Came the Yaksha tried and true;
Warrior Arjun, faithful Yaksha,
Found a true friend, each in each,
For the pure are quick in trusting,
And their love not far to reach.

VI

As a darkness fills Sumeru
When the god of day departs,
Parting from the warrior Arjun
Filled with grief his brothers' hearts;
But dispelled by sense of duty,—
Though so bitter was their lot,—
Sorrow in the royal brothers
Yielded to a higher thought;
Hope and trust in Arjun's prowess,
Hatred of the common foe,
Confidence in brighter future,
Quelled the sense of present woe.
Shadows leave the hours of daylight,
Seek the stillness of the night,—

Draupadi's lament

Sorrows left the warlike brothers,
Filled Draupadi in their might;
And as snow-flakes fill the lotus
Rising tear-drops filled her eye,
But to weep were inauspicious,
Though her bosom heaved a sigh.
Look of tenderness and sadness
Did her woman's glances send,
As a dear and sad memento
To a loved and parting friend;
And her heart was wrung by anguish,
Like a creeper rent and broke,
And her voice was choked by tear drops,
Sad her accents as she spoke.

VII

"Sole restorer of our glory,
Now, alas, in darkness lost,
Let thy manly heart and purpose
By no saddening thought be crost;
For in quest of fame and glory,
And of deeds which records fill,
Fortune ever leans to heroes
Labouring with a dauntless will!
Kings in glory rule the wide earth,
Conquering foemen in the strife,
We have lost that kingly glory
Dear to warrior as his life,
Till the chiefs of distant regions
Doubting heard our tale of shame,
Staining all our former valour
And our world-embracing fame!

Draupadi's anger

Tale of shame which dims our future,
Hides each deed of valour done,
As the shadow of the evening
Hides the glimmers of the sun,—
Tale of wrong and bitter insult
Rankling like a cruel smart,
And the thought of pain will freshen
When, O Arjun, thou shalt part!
Like a wounded forest-monarch
Changed thou art, thy glory faded,
Void of pride and pomp and prowess
Like the day by darkness shaded;
And the arms that once bedecked thee
Long unused have lost their gleam,
Form of pride hath changed and withered,
Like the summer's dwindled stream!
By these tresses, young Duhsasan
Dragged me to the council hall,
Still unbraided, powerless Arjun,
They remind thee of thy fall!
What is *Kshatra*,—true-born warrior,—
If he fails to help and save,
What is *Karmuk*,—bow of battle,—
If it fails the true and brave?
Vain thy virtues, mute thy glory,
And inglorious is thy might,
Or partaking of our sorrow
Do they imitate our plight?

VIII

"But they rashly tempt thee, Arjun,—
Lion's wrath the hunters shun,—

Drau-padi's farewell

Duty for thy worth elects thee
As the day elects the sun!
For a hero's deed of valour
Fills the glorious rolls of fame,
And a hero's name is foremost
When they count each warlike name;
Be a hero in thy striving,
And if sometimes in thee rise
Thoughts of sadness and of sorrow,
Indra helps the brave and wise!
Free from every secret evil
Do thy penance lone and long,
Guard thee from each lurking danger,
Secret foe who smites the strong;
Duty calls thee! Part we, Arjun,
Do the Saint's behest in peace,
And our dearest hopes fulfilling
Seek once more our dear embrace!"

IX

Thus spake Drupad's daughter
Rousing Arjun's wrath,
He was like the red sun
In the northern path;
And his mighty weapons
Manfully he wore,
Like a spell terrific
Form of terror bore!
Bow the dread of foemen,
Arrows keen and dread,
And the well-filled quiver,
And the shining blade,

Arjun parts

And the gem-wrought armour,
Like the star-wrought sky,
On his deep-scarred person
Donned the warrior high!
Guided by the Yaksha
To the hills he went,
Hermits filled with sorrow
Pious wishes sent;
And the sky breathed music,
Flowers fell from above,
And the ocean's breakers
Clasped the earth in love!

BOOK III

ARJUN'S PENANCE

Arjun followed the advice of Vyasa, and engaged in a long and arduous penance to win celestial arms. The news of the devotions of the unknown worshipper, armed like a warrior, were carried to Indra, the god of sky.

I

ARJUN, bent on mighty penance,
Followed Ganga's rocky course,
Scaled the hills, as Vishnu mounted
Golden bird that heavenward soars.
Forest trees like holy hermits
Sang his praise by hum of bees,
Bent their heads to yield their blossoms,
Shaken by the gentle breeze.

Mountain streams and woods

And the woodland-scented zephyr,
    Saturate with Ganga's spray,
Blew on Arjun's face and forehead,
    Clasped them in their amorous play.
And the mountain torrent's music,
    And the forest's mingled cry,
Stirred his heart like beat of war-drum,
    Waked in him a purpose high!

II

Wild cascades and rolling rivers
    Broke the tall tree in their course,
But the gentle creeper bending
    Escaped their all-resistless force.
Tuneful birds arose before him,
    And with voices filled the brake,
Filled the bosom of the waters,
    Spread a mantle on the lake!
Elephants in deeper jungle
    Marked the hills with many a scar,
And the moisture from their temples
    Drew the wild bees from afar.
On the lake the golden Chakwa
    Mingled in the wave of gold,
Till the wild cry of the female
    Jealous love and anguish told.
Varying tints upon the waters
    Shewed the gems that hidden lay,
As the blushes of the maiden
    Secrets of the heart betray!
Till the rising mountain tempest
    Broke the waters' silver sheen,

Mountain rills flowing into the Ganges

And the foam like Ketak blossoms,
Whitened all the woodland scene!

III

Arjun marked the spots of brightness
Floating on the water's sheen,—
Oily creatures of the streamlets
Gambolled in the caves within;
And he saw the shells of mountains
Lying on the rocky bed,—
Drops of beauty in them glistened,
Were they tears in sorrow shed?
Creepers bloomed in shoots of crimson,
Sparkling in the dew-drop's glow,—
Calling to the eye of lovers
Lips of red and teeth of snow!
Tuskers gambolled in the waters,
Frolicked in the streamlets fair,
And the perfume from their temples
Lent a fragrance to the air;
And the scaly water serpent
Often darted in the air,
Breathed its poisoned breath in bubbles
White as cloudlets soft and fair;
And the fishes glanced and sparkled,
Quick as woman's glances bold,
And as maids wait on their princess,
Streams to Ganga's waters rolled!

IV

Arjun scaled a spacious upland,
Found a spot alone, apart,

Graced by many a flower of forest,
 Pure as purity of heart;
And the creepers starred with blossoms,
 Trees where fruits in clusters hung,
Bent the heart of pious Arjun
 To his penance deep and long;
And by rules he fixed his purpose
 On the rites which hermits know,
What though arduous his devotions,
 Faith of heart can conquer woe!
Quelling every earthly passion,
 Cleansing sin by holy light,
Arjun rose in righteous merit
 Like the waxing moon of night!
By his ceaseless contemplation
 Cravings of the flesh he stilled,
Till a perfect peace and calmness
 Arjun's steadfast bosom filled;—
Till by hymns and high devotion
 He had won the highest grace,
And within him dwelt harmonious
 Matchless power and mighty peace!

Arjun begins his penance in a lonely spot

V

Arjun wore his plaited tresses,
 Red as anchorites should wear,—
As the tall trees wear their foliage
 Crimsoned by the sunbeams fair;
Girt in arms, but calm and saint-like,
 Gentle, but august and tall,—
Forest creatures knew his kindness
 Love of heart endeareth all!

Nature is auspicious to his penance

Softly on him blew the breezes,
Shed a fragrance as they went,
Fiery sun forgot his glamour
And a chastened radiance lent;
And when Arjun plucked the blossoms
Stately trees bent down their head,
Earth put forth her softest mantle
For the hero's nightly bed!
Cloudless sky to him auspicious
Sent its showers the dust to lay,
Kindly nature helped his penance,
Nursed the hermit night and day;
And the blossom of his fortune
Thus its glorious fruitage bore,—
But these signs changed not his ardour,
Calm and changeless evermore!

VI

Indra's menials in the forest
Witnessed Arjun's rites severe,
Of his penance long and lonesome
Spake to Indra in their fear;
And before the Thunder-Wielder
Gently their obeisance made,
And in soft and humble accents
Of the unknown hermit said.

VII

"Like a bright star of the sky,
Clad in barks on yonder hill,
One, intent on purpose high,
Doth his rites,—and earth is still!

Indra's menials convey tidings of his penance

Arms whose muscles snake-like coil
Hold an ever bended bow,—
But all gentle are his deeds,
Gentler soul lives not below!
Winds blow soft, the sward is green,
Grateful rains the dust allay,
Elements by worth subdued
In accord obeisance pay!
Forest beasts their strife forget,
Listen to his beck and word,
Trees on him with blossoms wait,
Mountains own him as their lord!
Penance speaks a purpose high,
Dauntless mein denotes success,—
Hermit, but a warrior too,
Who he be, we may not guess!
If from saints he counts descent,
Or from warlike kingly line,—
Who can tell, or why in woods
He performs his rites divine;
If he toils for purpose pure,
If for empire, who can guess,—
Foresters are poor in sense,
Thou must know, and thou canst bless!

BOOK IV

THE ADVENT OF INDRA

The god Indra was pleased with Arjun's penance, came to visit him in disguise, and counselled him to worship Siva.

I

Indra comes disguised as an old anchorite

ARJUN by his arduous penance
Won a hermit's holy fame,
Till unto his forest-dwelling
Indra in his mercy came;
Came disguised,—as come the bright gods,—
Like an ancient anchorite,
Wearied by a tiresome journey,
Weak in limbs and weak in sight.
And his red locks closely plaited
With his white hair mingling fell,
As the evening's crimson radiance
Mingles with the moonbeams pale;
And his eyes bedimmed in lustre,
And by fleecy eye-brows shaded,
Were like winter's withered lotus
By a snow fall pale and faded.
Yet he seemed, albeit so slender,
Still instinct with strength of life,
Like an old man hale and hearty,
Nourished by a careful wife!
Thus concealed came mighty Indra
Radiant still with heavenly light,
As the sun is hid but faintly
By a cloud-bank, fleecy white;

Indra greets Arjun

With a grace divine he glittered
Though so ancient and so hoary,
Spreading o'er the hills and woodlands
Lustre of his shaded glory!
Him the pious Arjun welcomed,
Greeted with a kind embrace,—
Sight of friends instils a pleasure
Though unknown to us their face;
Indra too received with gladness
Homage which to guests is paid,
On a seat of wild grass rested,
And in gentle accents said.

II

"Well hast thou in early age
Choice of hermit's duties made,
Aged mortals like myself
Oft by worldly thoughts are led;
And thy deep devotions, youth,
Unto higher life will lead,
Grace of form we often meet
Grace of heart is rare indeed!
Transient as the autumn cloud
Pride and pomp of human kind,
Pleasures please us for a day,
Bitter sorrows leave behind;
Mortals' days are full of ills,
Unseen comes the hand of Death,
Holy work alone endures,
Faith survives the fleeting breath;
Wisely therefore hast thou chosen
Rites to bright Immortals dear,

Questions him about his war-like guise

But, despite thy pious penance,
Thy attire inspires my fear!

III

"Skins and barks of forest trees
Suit the holy anchorite,
Wherefore then in warlike guise
Wearest thou this armour bright?
If devoid of vain desires
In the righteous path wouldst go,
Wherefore then, misguided youth,
Quivers and this mighty bow?
If thy holy penance bids
Angry thoughts and passions cease,
Doth this sword, like arm of Death,
Lead thy restless heart to peace?
Much I fear, against some foe
Seekest thou a vengeance dire,
Warriors deal in deadly arms,
Hermits nurse the Holy Fire.
He who sighs for warlike fame
Soils the hermits' holy rite,
As the fool with hands impure
Soils the spring, pellucid, bright.
Therefore chase this lust of glory,
For it drives to sinful deeds,
Casts a stain on stainless virtue,
And from holy peace misleads.

IV

"Listen more! Who strives for fame
Wins on earth a brief success,

Condemns lust of fame and worldly desires

But as rivers end in seas,
    Ends in trouble and distress.
Wealth is won by evil ways,
    Leads to thoughts and things unclean,
Riches bring us cark and care,
    End in suffering and in sin.
Impure pleasures, earthly joys,
    Stifle strong and steadfast faith,
And like snakes with poisoned fangs
    Sting the heedless unto death!
Fickle Fortune, ever quick,
    Loves not with a constant will,—
Fools her fleeting favours seek,
    Chasing shapeless shadows still!
Fortune,—if she spurned the weak,
    On her fame it were no stain,—
But the constant and the strong,
    Likewise earn the maid's disdain!
Love is still an emptier shade
    Vanishing in life-long woe,—
Sad bereavement, young heart's death,
    Bitter pang on earth below.
When we meet the loved and true,
    Lonely places peopled seem,
Penury hath charms to please,
    Grief itself is happy dream.
When we lose the loved and true,
    Bright hopes vanish and delude,
Life is like a poisoned dart,
    Company is solitude!

Counsels striving after eternal bliss and salvation

V

" Thus each fleeting thing of earth
Ends in sorrow and in grief,
Righteousness alone endures,
Faith alone brings true relief;
For our life is brief and vain,
Pleasures please us for a day,
Holy work survives our breath,
Turn not from the righteous way!
Stain not, youth, these sacred rites
With the lust of fame and war,
Seek the path of lasting bliss,
Leaving earthly things afar;
Conquer lust of earthly things
Born with mortals at their birth,
Conquest of thy inner self
Is the conquest of the earth!
Weak are they and narrow-souled,
Worldly power who seek to wield,
Slaves of passion, slaves of lust,
Even like cattle of the field!
Joys that pleased thee yesterday
Ghost-like haunt the vacant mind,
Pleasures fly like fleeting light,
Leave a deeper gloom behind!
Ever wished but unobtained,
Cherished but to cause us pain,
Never present never gone,
Happiness on earth is vain!
On this lofty mountain range,
Where the Ganga wanders far,
Strive for thy salvation, youth,
Leave this impure lust of war!"

VI

Arjun replies to Indra

Indra thus in guise of hermit
　　Spake his thoughts and paused awhile,
And in humble words but forceful
　　Arjun answered with a smile.
"Full of weight and wisdom, father,
　　Is thy counsel to my ear,
Full of sense and deepest import
　　Is thy utterance calm and clear;
Like an independent Sastra
　　In its reasons strong in sooth,
Like the Vedas sung by Rishis
　　Mighty in its holy truth;
In its ample force inviolate
　　Like the vast inviolate sea,
Gentle in its soft persuasion
　　Like a soul from passions free!
He who utters words so noble
　　Is a saint of spotless birth,
He who harbours thoughts so peaceful
　　Glasses heaven upon this earth!
But, unknown to thee, my father,
　　Is the purpose of my rites,
Hence in accents soft and gentle
　　Speakest thou of anchorites;
Even the god of speech will falter
　　Speaking of a thing unknown,
Even the highest effort fails us
　　By our blindness overthrown!

VII

"Father, thy advice is holy,
　　But, alas, it suits not me,

Narrates the story of Yudhishthir's fall

As the radiant stars of midnight
Do not suit the light of day!
I am of the race of Kshatra,
Pandu's son, of Pritha born,
And I serve my honoured elder
Of his realm and glory shorn;
And I do this holy penance
As by saintly Vyasa told,
For to please the Thunder-Wielder
By these rites prescribed of old.
Fate's decree is stern and woeful,
Mortals' bliss is often crossed,
Now his realm and wife my elder
Staked on game of dice,—and lost;
And in evenings long and dreary,
Grieving at their doleful fate,
His fair queen and faithful brothers
Term of my devotions wait.
From our backs they tore the garments,
Shamed us in the palace hall,
Pierced our souls, th' exulting foemen,
With their insults on our fall;
And in presence of the chieftains
Dragged our chaste and spotless queen,
Death has sealed a vow of vengeance
For that insult fierce and keen!
False Duhsasan base of purpose
Held the dame so pure of mind,
As the gnarled tree of forest
Holds its lengthening shade behind;
Vain she looked upon her husband
In her sorrow deep and high,
Pride and anguish tore her bosom,

And of Draupadi's disgrace

Checked the tear-drop in her eye !
True to plighted word, he suffered
Insults keen and words unkind,—
What is conquest of an empire
To such conquest of the mind ?
Noble souls retain their calmness
Though by grief and passions riven,
As the ocean keeps its confines
Though by raging tempest driven !
Friendship with our faithless kinsmen
To this shame and insult led,—
Death awaits the man who slumbers
'Neath a falling bank for shade ;
Men who fear no sinful action,
Right from wrong who do not see,—
Who can guess their artful purpose,
Who can fathom Fate's Decree ?

VIII

" Shamed, insulted by our foemen,
Sure this heart had ceased to beat,
But I hoped this arm of vengeance
Would inflict requital meet ;
Shamed, insulted by our foemen,
Low as cattle on the plain,
Scarce we see each other's faces,
Dare not meet the eyes of men !
Humbled by the loss of glory
In the woods our days we pass,
Mortals when bereft of honour
Are like low and trodden grass ;
But survey those snowy summits
By no living creature crossed,

Proclaims his thirst for revenge

Loftiness is highest virtue,
    Honour is our highest boast!
Fickle Fortune frowns or favours,
    Changeless lives a hero's fame,
And the name of man befits him
    When true glory decks his name;
Highest he in rolls of honour
    Who hath toiled and earned his meed,
And the finger of the reckoner
    Points to none of worthier deed!
Even this range of lofty mountains
    May be crossed by living wight,
But the man of truth and valour
    Is inviolate in his might;
And his race and land he brightens,
    Fills the wide earth with his light,
And his glory's bright effulgence
    Pales the radiant Queen of Night;
And his wrath like flash of lightning
    Smites the false and crouching slave,
And his fame through untold ages
    Lives among the true and brave!

IX

"Hence I seek not wealth or pleasure,
    Fleeting as the torrent's flow,
Nor, afraid of death and danger,
    Crave the grace the gods bestow;
But I seek to wash the insult,—
    Stain for which this heart hath bled,—
With the tear-drops for our foemen
    By their sorrowing widows shed!

And his determination to act as a man

If this hope on which I've rested,
Be unreal, idle, vain,
Be it so;—thy words are wasted,
Pardon if I cause thee pain;
Till I conquer all my foemen,
Win again our long lost fame,
Vain to me are joys celestial,—
Hindrance to my lofty aim!
For the warrior lives not, breathes not,
Or is dead like trodden grass,
Who will let his good sword slumber
While his fame and glory pass;
Whose warm blood flows not in anger
When his foemen steal his fame,
Dost thou, man of peace and virtue,
Give him warrior's noble name?
Vainly he assumes the title
While his right arm wins no meed,
Sacred is the honoured title
Sanctified by manlike deed;
For, whose name in wonder spoken
Pales the names of other men,
And whose deeds are sung by nations,
He is MAN among all men!

X

"Listen more! Our honoured elder,
Vowing retribution fell,
Waits my help as thirsty trav'ller
Waits beside the cooling well;
Heedless of my elder's wishes,
Heedless of his life and peace,

Announces that he will win his object or die in the endeavour

Can I shirk this task of honour
False unto my creed and race?
Wherefore preachest to me, father,
Life retired before my time,
Sages live the life in forest
Not in youth but after prime;
Love of mother, love of brothers,
Duty to my elder's wife,
Warrior's task explained by Vyasa,—
All forbid a forest-life!
Honour's maxims, gentle hermit,
Brace the soldier for the fight,
Not retirement is his duty,
But to battle for the right;
Let me therefore on these mountains
Until death pursue my aim,
Or by gracious Indra's succour
Live to win our long lost fame!"

XI

Arjun spake with fervour
Thoughts that filled his mind,
Indra heard with gladness
And with feelings kind;
And the Thunder-Wielder
Wore his form divine,
Bade the prince to penance
Still his heart incline.
"Unto mighty Siva
Do thy homage pay,
He alone can help thee
In the dubious fray;

Indra advises Arjun to pray to Siva

Peerless in thy prowess,
    Matchless in thy might,
Win the arms of Siva,
    Conquer in the fight!"

BOOK V

THE ADVENT OF SIVA

Arjun followed the advice of Indra, and pleased Siva by his penance. Siva appeared before Arjun in the guise of a hunter.

1

Once again, by Indra's mandate,
    Arjun did his pious rites,
Rendered worship unto Siva
    Dwelling in Kailasa's heights!
Firm in faith and pure in purpose,
    Tireless 'neath the summer sun,
Moveless in the blast of winter,
    Mightier penance he begun;
Mortifying flesh and senses,
    Lonely in his lofty bower,
Arjun still pursued his duty,—
    High resolve hath wond'rous power!
Luscious fruit that ripened near him,
    Crystal rill that rippled by,—
Faith is food unto the righteous,—
    Drew from him nor wish nor sigh.
Pale despair nor pride of virtue
    Ever dimmed his sacred toil,

His greatness and glory

Lust of flesh nor impure passions
    Did his steadfast penance soil.
And he wore a matchless glory,
    Though subdued by rigid rite,
Trembling hermits marked his prowess,—
    Great in heart are great in might!
Brighter than the mighty wood-fire
    Shone his light in forests still,—
Faith is mightier than the ocean,
    Loftier than the towering hill!
And his hymns as Arjun chanted,
    And his rites as he begun,
Beamed upon his face a radiance
    Like the halo of the sun!

II

Clad in armour dark, he carried
    Mighty bow across his chest,—
So the wood-clad darksome mountain
    Wears the rainbow on its breast!
And when for his day's ablutions
    Arjun walked in morning hour,
Solid mountains felt his footsteps,—
    Holy worth is wondrous power!
Aye, a lustre fell upon him,
    As he stood serene and high,
Till the firmament it lighted,
    Flashed unto the upper sky!
And on moonless nights around him
    Played a softer gentler ray,
Like the soft and silver moonbeams
    Changing darkness into day!

But at morn so bright his radiance,
That the paler orb or sun,
Pacing through a sky of azure,
Scarce with wonted lustre shone!

Holy Saints convey tidings of his penance to Siva

III

Holy saints beheld in awe
Arjun with his bow unbent,—
"Is this Siva's self,"—they asked,
"On some Titan's death intent?
Is he Indra or the Sun,
God of Fire who helps our rites,—
Strength like his no mortals own,
Faith like his no anchorites!"
But unlike the flaming Fire
All serene was Arjun's light,
And unlike the scorching Sun
Gentle was his holy might!
Lost in doubt the holy saints
In their fear to Siva press,
So all virtues come to Peace,
So all faiths to Righteousness!

IV

Blinded by the Holy Ray,—
By the God's effulgent Light,—
Vain they sought with mortal eyes
To discern his radiant might;
Till by hymns they humbly sought
Him, the Lord of time and space,
And from Siva's eye and front
Flowed to them his godlike grace.

Siva standing on the snow-clad mountains

Resting on his sacred bull
Ashen arm of wondrous might,
He,—by Uma sought and loved,—
Stood upon the mountain's height!
Far from creatures of the earth
Stood where snow-clad mountains tower,
But the ocean, land, and sky
Felt his presence and his power!
Coiling serpents stretched their length
Round the muscles of his feet,
As upon broad-bosomed earth
Rocky ranges cross and meet;
On his blue and ample throat
Twining *Nagas* white as snow,
Like the thread of twice-born men,
Caught its dark and tremulous glow!
By his tresses partly hid
Young moon's glistening crescent hung,
And like Ganga's sparkling wave
Silver radiance softly flung;
And he listened as the saints
Hymns and holy lays addressed,
Telling how a mortal's rites
Filled the wide earth with unrest!

V

"Listen to us, mighty Lord,
How a man with Titan's might
Quells the earth with righteous toil,
Pales the sun with brighter light;
Bow he wears and shining darts,
Armour and a wond'rous blade,

Siva explains the cause of Arjun's penance

Yet in hermit's skin and bark,
    Peaceful toils the warrior dread!
When he treads, the broad earth quakes,
    When he prays, the forests glow,
Starry skies are hushed and still,
    And the breezes cease to blow;
When at morn he climbs the hill
    Stillness falls on earth and air,—
What great task, what deed unknown,
    May his lofty purpose dare?
If he seeks to rule the earth,
    Or destroy it in his ire,
If he toils to win the sky,
    None may guess his object dire;
Thou alone must know it, Lord,
    For no secret blinds thine eye,
Thou dost know and thou canst save,
    Thou canst help and thou art nigh."

VI

Unto them then Siva answered
    In his accents full of grace,—
Deep as voice of mighty ocean
    Sounding to the ends of space!
"Know ye, who with lofty penance
    Worships in Badrika's heath,—
Earth-born man but part of VISHNU
    Who is Life and who is Death!
And he toils in rites enduring
    Foes to conquer and to quell,—
Foes whose dark deeds fill the wide earth,
    And whose crimes the heavens assail!

Siva assumes the guise of a hunter

By the will of ancient BRAHMA
Krishna took his human birth,—
With brave Arjun,—to accomplish
Heaven's high mandate on the earth;
But the wily Titan Muka,
Foe of bright gods of the sky,
Seeks to smite the pious Arjun,
Seeks to thwart our purpose high;
Yet to slay the warrior-hermit
Openly to try were vain,—
Muka wears the shape of wild-boar
His unrighteous end to gain!
I will take the form of hunter
Pierce the wild boar in the heart,—
Arjun is a valiant sportsman,
He will doubtless send his dart;
Pale with fasts and rigid penance
Still he owns a wond'rous might,—
Ere the mortal wins my favour
He must prove his worth in fight!"

VII

As the bright gods come,
Siva came disguised,—
Hunter's paint he wore,
Hunter's toil he prized;
And with tendrils twined
Fell his shaggy hair,
Peacock's radiant plume
Decked his eye-brows fair;
Bows and arrows keen
Glittered in his hand,

Marches with his band through mountain forests

Like a lurid cloud
    Siva led his band!
And his armèd host
    Waited on his word,
And like hunters held
    Bow and lance and sword;
Sweeping through the woods,
    Scouring o'er the wold,
Filling earth with sounds
    Marched the huntsmen bold!
Scream of bird and beast
    Echoed through the land,
Woods and mountains quaked
    At the forest band;
Beast and bird forgot
    Hate and mutual strife,
Danger made them friends,
    And their fear of life!
Chowris fain would fly
    Startled by the yell,
But the bush and briar
    Caught their flowing tail;
Lion, king of woods,
    Owned no dastard fear,
Marked the hunters pass
    Calmly from his lair!
Fish leaped from the lake,
    Beasts stood on its shore,
Rills were stained by trees
    Which the tuskers tore;
Buffaloes from woods
    Broke through tangled trees,
Wild flowers with their scent

Comes to Arjuna's hermitage

Filled the fragrant breeze;
Splashing through the stream,
Dashing o'er the heath,
Wild beasts tore the woods
Like the tempest's breath!
Past the forest wild,
Hunters came and stood,
Where the peaceful deer
Browsed in Arjun's wood;
And they witnessed Muka
From a covert rise,
Tearing earth with tusks
In a boar's disguise;
Leaving by the lake
All his armèd force,
Siva all alone
Tracked the wild boar's course!

BOOK VI

PRAYER AND BLESSING

A boar was killed, and a combat ensued between the rival huntsmen, Siva and Arjun, over the game. Siva was pleased with the valour and determination of the hermit-warrior, and gave him the celestial arms which he sought.

I

PLEASED with Arjun's worth and valour,
Grace of soul and strength of arm,
Siva clasped the dauntless mortal
And assumed his godlike form!

Arjun's sublime hymn to Siva

Gentle rain from clouds descended,
    Fragrant blossoms fell from high,
And a soft celestial music
    Floated from th' auspicious sky!
Indra and the bright Immortals
    Viewed with joy the mortal's might,
And their cars of light and lustre
    Gemmed the sky like stars at night!
Heavenly swans with sweet bills tinkling
    Drew the chariots through the air,
Sailed across the sea of azure
    On their pinions soft and fair!
Softly, gently, reverently,
    Grateful Arjun bent his head,
And in pure and pious accents
    To the Bright Immortal prayed.

II

"Lord of Grace! The World's Asylum!
    Whom by worship we attain,
Saints have conquered Death's destruction,
    Shewed Thy path to gods and men!
Whoso seeks Thee not in worship,
    Shunned by dearest kith and kin,
Lives a life of vain illusion,
    Dies a death of woe and sin;
Whoso seeks Thee in affection,
    Breaks through ills that wait our birth,
Finds in Thee his true salvation,
    Peace and bliss unknown on earth!
Some are lured by worldly pleasures,
    Some for heaven's enjoyments sigh,—

Siva's blessings and gift of arms

Save in Thee no true salvation
Is there in the earth or sky;
For in Thee alone is refuge,
And who leaves Thee dies in woe,—
This is Law, and not Thy anger,
Wrath nor passion dost Thou know!
Thee we serve with tainted worship,
And Thy form we darkly guess,—
Even thus our soul's blind longings
Have the power to heal and bless;
For illusions mock our vision,
Shadow-like our actions flee,—
He sees true who sees Thy image,
He acts true who acts in Thee!
Divers teachers often teach us
Divers precepts wise and great,
But Thy grace and blessing only
From our bonds can liberate;
And to rid this world of troubles,
Sin and sorrow, stress and storm,
Various forms at will Thou wearest,
Thou art Mercy—without form!"

III

Arjun reverently
Did His mercy crave,
He unto the warrior
Heavenly blessing gave;
And the gift of Siva
With a radiant flame,
As the sun to rain-cloud,
Unto Arjun came!

The gods prophesy Arjun's success

All the gods assembled
    Blessed the man of truth,
Gave him arms celestial
    Spake unto the youth.
"Thou hast proved thee faithful,
    Thou shalt win thy end,
To the man true-hearted
    Gods their succour send!"
Thus they blessed and vanished,
    Arjun came and stood
Once more by his brothers
    In the Dwaita wood;
And the good Yudhishthir
    Blessed the emprise done,
For by truth and valour
    Destiny is won!

The translations in the present volume of the Temple Classics are the work of Mr Romesh Chundra Dutt, *who has previously translated for the series the two great epics of Ancient India.* Mr Dutt *has also revised the proofs and added the Marginalia.*

BEDFORD STREET, LONDON,
September 1905.

Turnbull & Spears, Printers, Edinburgh.